Small Business
Marketing
Your Ultimate Guide

By Jimmy Nicholas

1st Edition 2013
Copyright © 2013 by JE2000, LLC

ISBN-13: 978-06157980-0-4
ISBN-10: 0615798004

Published by JE2000, LLC
86 Boston Post Road #3, Waterford, CT 06385

Jimmy Nicholas
www.JimmyMarketing.com

Edited by Jennifer-Crystal Johnson
www.jennifercrystaljohnson.com

Printed in the United States of America

To my always supportive wife, Jennifer, who believed in me,
even when she had no proof she should. I will be forever grateful for your 110% trust and support. Thank You!

To my mother and father, Jane and Joe, who always believed in me, even when I didn't believe in myself. You taught me to dream big and never quit until I reach my dreams, and then dream bigger. I will be forever grateful for your unconditional love and support. You molded me into the man I am today. Thank You!

To the thousands of clients I have worked with over the years, who trusted my knowledge and strategies to help their organizations grow and succeed. I am always grateful for your continued support. Thank You!

To my team at Jimmy Marketing and EasyWebCreations.com, who supported me and continue to support me in our journey of accomplishing our mission of helping organizations grow and succeed. Thank You!

To my mentors, coaches, peers, and friends who have supported me during my journey of building multiple successful brands and companies. We missed out on some fun times while I was focused on building companies, but you still supported me. Thank You!

To the readers of this book, who may just be starting out in business or who may already be operating a thriving business, I hope this book helps your organization continue to grow and succeed. While the path to success wasn't easy for me, I hope this book will save you some steps and struggle on your way to the top. Thank You!

Table of Contents

Foreword
By Fireman Mike LeMoine

The student becomes the teacher.

I had just gotten off stage after speaking to over 800 business owners about how to effectively use the Internet for marketing their businesses. When I speak, I am known as "Fireman Mike." I am a firefighter who began figuring out this Internet stuff and started helping businesses. I received some attention and before I knew it, I was speaking on national stages to large groups of people seeking my advice.

Usually as a speaker, when you get offstage everyone crowds around, pictures are taken and questions are answered. This time seemed no different than the others.

However, what was different was a few days later I received a video from a guy named Jimmy Nicholas. He was on the golf course and shot me a "thank you video" for my talk. I immediately thought, "WOW! This guy is different, he gets it!"

A few months later the same guy bought a marketing product and I began coaching and helping him with his business. I recalled the video he had sent me, and how different he seemed from others I had worked with.

I quickly realized that what makes Jimmy different is his hunger to learn and his eagerness to implement what he has learned. I was amazed when we talked, just a short time later, at how much progress he had made.

Jimmy was helping his clients in a BIG way with their marketing and had even developed an entire software platform.

As Jimmy began sharing with me what he was working on and how it would impact businesses and marketing, I was awestruck.

This was the moment I knew that the student had just become the teacher.

Since that time, I have not only learned a ton from Jimmy, but have been fortunate enough to also work with him on several business ventures as well. Jimmy's knowledge of marketing and how to apply that marketing to a business is amazing. Every time I am with him, I find myself taking notes.

Many of the things I have taken notes on are in this book.

This book is not just a book to sit and read for pleasure. This is a book you should read with a notebook and a highlighter. This book is filled with insights and knowledge that you need to know, NOW!

Jimmy has taken his knowledge and expertise, put it into this book, and is GIVING you what has taken him years of work to learn and perfect. This book is an encyclopedia of knowledge about marketing that is not just theory, but real world tactics and strategies that will ignite your marketing and bring customers in the door.

We both know that the landscape for businesses has changed. No longer are people grabbing the phone book to find your business. They are online, they are on their mobile phones, and they are overwhelmed. You must be online and have proven ways to be in front of them in order to get their attention and to get new customers.

As you read this book you will quickly see there are a ton of things you can be doing to market your business better. Jimmy is truly a master marketer who understands the needs of a business. More importantly, he is a man of integrity who you can trust to tell it to you straight and provide you with the information that is vital to making a difference in your business.

Get ready to become a student again because class is in session and Jimmy is ready to teach you a ton of valuable information in this book.

Introduction
How to Read This Book

Hi! My name is Jimmy Nicholas, and I'd like to personally welcome you to a positive and educational experience for you and your business. By purchasing this book, you've taken the first step toward learning important information about marketing, sales, how to create a marketing plan, how to implement it, and by doing all of this, how to increase the success of your business.

Since I started my business in 1997, I've seen returns of over 1,235% by designing marketing structures that work. As part of my own expanding small business, this book will provide exactly how and what I do to get such high returns on my marketing and advertising efforts.

This book is designed as a map. More than that, you can think of it as a marketing atlas. I'll show you each step of the way what you need to do in order to grow your business, from the brainstorming and planning process all the way to the maintenance process after initial implementation.

Mark the pages you find useful. Take action as you're reading. Do some of the activities mentioned in the book. Use a highlighter. There's a lot to learn and a lot of information to share, so do what you need to in order to keep that knowledge handy. Also, make sure you can easily reference information you'll need at a later date, without the distraction of shuffling through pages. Your time is valuable!

I recommend starting at chapter fourteen. Chapter fourteen summarizes the key points of each chapter. Then, come back to this page and continue reading. After reading chapters one through fourteen, re-read chapter fourteen. This process will help you learn the strategies discussed throughout the book.

Additionally, use this book as a reference and use the table of contents when you want to read more about a particular topic.

I encourage you to learn everything you possibly can from this book by taking notes, marking pages, and referencing what you need when you need it. It's important to know, every single topic described in this book is something we implement and have seen success with. If you'd like our help with anything described in this book, please visit www.JimmyMarketing.com or call us toll-free at 877-253-0273.

ADDITIONAL RESOURCES EXCLUSIVE TO THE READERS OF THIS BOOK!

Because I believe in providing value and teaching others marketing basics, my team and I have put together additional chapters and resources to help small business owners, just like you get the most from their marketing endeavors, as well as having a team of people who can help along the way.

We have combined the best content from both Jimmy Marketing, our online and offline marketing company, and EasyWebCreations.com, our dedicated website design division, to bring you additional resources that will help you convert suspects into prospects and then prospects into clients.

VISIT www.JimmysGift.com or CALL 877-253-0273 TO CLAIM YOUR ADDITIONAL RESOURCES TO LEARN & IMPLEMENT THE STRATGIES REVEALED IN THIS BOOK EVEN QUICKER!

LIMITED QUANTITIES AVAILBLE

The additional resources include reports, audio CDs, videos, invitations to webinars, seminars, one-on-one training, and more, absolutely FREE to our readers!

The additional resources are for the established business or a startup! If you are looking to increase your profits, while working less by implementing strategic marketing systems, these additional resources are for you.

This information could be worth hundreds of thousands, or even millions of dollars to your organization. To claim these additional resources, fill out the quick form on our website, www.JimmysGift.com or call 877-253-0273. You'll start receiving this valuable information right away.

www.JimmysGift.com
877-253-0273

Chapter One
Jimmy's Story

Before we get right into the marketing strategies you should be implementing into your business, I want to share where I came from and my story with you. From selling baseball cards to walking two miles to cut someone's lawn as a child, I have always been very entrepreneurial.

In 1997, when I was 15 years old, I saw a Yellow Pages book on my desk. Since the Internet was just starting, I decided to start calling businesses and see if they needed a website. After about 250 "no's" and hang ups, a local jewelry store owner said, "Sure! Come on over and give me a presentation." I said, "Of course!" I ran upstairs and asked my mom to drive me over to the jewelry store. Remember, I was 15 and couldn't drive. Thankfully, she agreed!

Neither my mom nor I realized she would be waiting for me in the car for over two hours. However, she said the smile on my face when I walked out of the store was all worth it. I did it. I sold my first website. I then realized, oh boy – now I better figure out how to build a website! As I learned about websites, I learned that every website needs to be on a server for a web hosting account with a domain registration in order for people to access it. Since I was in high school, I didn't have the time on my hands to continue to design and develop websites. So I decided to shift my focus and build a web hosting company. I grew the hosting company by using Google Adwords to attract clients from all over the world.

After I graduated from Bryant University in Smithfield, Rhode Island in 2003, I knew I had more time on my hands again and decided to diversify and start offering website design. In 2004, I went from operating out of my dorm room to setting up an office in my parents' basement. In 2005, my wife and I purchased our home and I moved the office into the basement of our new home. In 2008, we moved into our first official office. And by we I mean me, my mom, and my first employee, Dave Costello.

At this point we were just offering website design and web hosting. As I brought on more team members, we needed room to expand. There were a couple of other offices in between then and our present location in Waterford.

In 2011, I was at a marketing conference in San Diego and was brought up on stage. When I was introduced, I was introduced as Jimmy. Now keep in mind I have been a James my entire life. You could imagine, at age 15 I was trying to be as formal as possible. Well, the emcee of the event started calling me Jimmy, Jimbo, Jimeriah, The Jimster, and ironically the name Jimmy stuck. After I was done speaking on stage, I immediately went on my mobile phone and saw that jimmymarketing.com was available, so I registered it.

Well, I have branded and invested hundreds of thousands of dollars into marketing EasyWebCreations.com. We were offering more than just websites, so it just made sense to start marketing Jimmy Marketing as the parent company, with EasyWebCreations.com as the web design division of Jimmy Marketing.

In 2012, we moved to our current location. We were able to layout and build the office to fit our needs from having a room dedicated to video, to a conference and training room, to offices for our team members. Today, we continue to expand our team and bring in top quality people that specialize in various aspects of marketing such as web design, search engine optimization, pay-per-click management, video marketing, reputation marketing, mobile marketing, social media management, direct mail, and so much more.

For more information about my story, visit www.AboutJimmy.com. I hope you enjoyed hearing my story. I would especially love to hear yours.

Chapter Two
What are your goals? What is your mission? What is a customer worth?

Read the above questions one more time and take a moment to think about them. Your customers are the lifeblood of your business; without them, there is nothing. Whether your customers are individuals or other businesses is irrelevant. They are all customers and they are immensely important to your business. In fact, I am a firm believer that there is no Business to Consumer (B to C), and no Business to Business (B to B). There is, however, People to People (P to P). In every organization there is a person that makes their buying decisions. This is an important point because we do not market to businesses, but always market to people.

Keeping this in mind, think about what your goals are for your business. You can certainly take yourself to greater heights by working hard and being diligent. Until you reach the audience who wants what your business provides, your efforts can only plateau after a while.

So how do you set goals and reach your audience while keeping everyone in mind? Let's take a closer look to fully address this issue.

Your marketing efforts need to be laser-focused in order to be effective. Did you know that people are exposed to over 5,000 marketing messages per day on average? Whew! That's a lot. Some people ask, how is that possible? Think of all the logos you see in a day, not to mention the actual paid advertising. Your marketing needs to get through the clutter and stand out to the people you're trying to reach: your target audience.

With the Internet being the best way to reach the highest number of people, it's a good idea to use social media and a website as a foundation for your marketing. This can then be paired with other marketing avenues like radio, newspaper, direct mail, and even the Yellow Pages.

The Yellow Pages?!

I know you're probably thinking the Yellow Pages are dying. You can still get positive returns with any media by making your marketing work together. By targeting the right audience with the right message, you will generate leads for your organization.

Let's take another look at the questions asked in this chapter's title.

What are your goals?

In order to plan anything, you have to have an endgame in mind. This is true for something as ordinary as a child's birthday party or as major as a company merger. Everything has to be planned, at least somewhat. Granted the merger would require a lot more detail than the party, but you get the idea.

Goal-setting is useful in your personal life, but it is absolutely *necessary* in your business. If you're running a business and don't have a purpose, then where are you running it to? It won't just get up and go by itself. You have to steer it in the direction you want it to go. That's where goal-setting and brainstorming come in.

People have all sorts of different ways to *set* goals. Every New Year's Day we see it all over the world: resolutions. But why do most people only limit their goal-setting to

January first? And why do so many people set their goals and never bother to follow through? It can be difficult, that's why!

But you're a business owner and have already experienced a number of setbacks, highs and lows, and ups and downs. Forget about setting goals. I want you to think of it more like creating a business plan.

A business plan is a lot like setting goals, just on a much larger and more detailed scale. I'm not saying that you have to create an entire business plan for your organization from scratch right now, but rather take the business plan that you created when you first began and look at it. Go ahead... dig it out, dust off the cobwebs, and take a look.

If you're like most business owners, especially if you're just starting out, you probably haven't looked at your business plan for months or even years. It's time to reconsider the business plan. It isn't just a document or ink on paper. A business plan is a living entity that can and should be updated, tweaked, changed, corrected, revised, and constantly evaluated.

Or maybe you never had a business plan. Many of the businesses I have worked with over the years never had a business plan and continue to successfully operate without one. However, I have found through my own experience that when I write out a plan either for my own company or for a client, I see things more clearly. The clients we write plans for agree as well. Once everything is on paper, there is a sense of security, clarity, and vision as to where the company is going. So, if you have never had a business plan, by actively going through this book and taking notes about what strategies you will implement into your business, you will have a marketing plan in place.

Just like a person, a business plan should grow and evolve. As you learn more about your business, marketing, expanding, and gain more insight into your industry, your business plan should see some of that valuable wisdom in its pages. The same is true for your marketing plan, which is what I'll be showing you how to create throughout the pages of this book.

Think about this, if you wanted to drive somewhere you have never been before, wouldn't you get there quicker and much more easily with directions or a map? It is the same in business. If you want to grow your business and want to take your business where it has never been before, a map is needed. Your map consists of a business plan.

Defining Your Mission

In growing my own company and through helping clients grow their businesses, I have found it most helpful to establish a clear mission. I am not a fan of long mission statements, but rather simple missions that make it easy for you and people on your team to adapt. Our mission is simple: we help organizations grow and succeed.

By constantly reminding our team of our mission, we have seen our culture evolve. With a simple mission, we now have a mission bigger than any specific task. When making decisions throughout the day, our team can reflect on our mission and it helps bring clarity to the direction of our business.

Additionally, I have found it exceptionally important to establish core values. Core values make it easier for our team to understand how I want people to think within our organization. Our core values are:

1. We have a "can-do" attitude.
2. We are experts in our field.
3. We provide a WOW experience.
4. We are passionate about results.
5. We have fun!

You may be wondering why I am including the importance of defining a mission and core values in this guide. Your mission and core values will not only shape your marketing and help you attract the type of clients you want to work with, but if you follow this guide, your business will grow and it will grow quickly. It is important to have your mission and core values in place prior to any major growth. In fact, defining your mission and core values will provide clarity and *help* you grow. Even if you are a one-person business, define your mission and core values.

What is a customer worth?

The days of the saying, "the customer is always right," seem to have dwindled to very few and far between. Many businesses often try to take advantage of customers and overcharge, and every day fake businesses start up for the sole purpose of running a scam.

It seems that society has forgotten that the customer *is* always right!

Think about it. Without your customers, you have no business. Without your business, you would just be one more person working hard to make someone else rich. So now I ask you one more time: what are your customers worth *to you?*

In my experience, a customer is priceless - especially if they are a repeat customer or send referrals your way. If you do your job well and run a customer-friendly company, you can multiply that repeat customer who sends referrals by thousands. That's a highly successful business!

To gain more customers, you need a marketing plan to reach out to the people who don't know you or your business. In order to reach a larger audience and gain more customers, you'll need to either advertise or market your business in a number of ways. This book will guide you in the right direction.

In the next chapter, I'll go over the importance of a marketing plan and help you create your very own marketing plan and marketing calendar.

Chapter Three
Creating a Marketing Plan with a Marketing Calendar

Let's get down to business. I've already explained a little bit about why marketing is important and why keeping your customers happy is absolutely required to run a successful business. Now, I'd like to go ahead and take that one step further and introduce you to the concept of creating a marketing plan with a marketing calendar, as well the reasons why this process is vital to growing and expanding your business.

Are you comfortable where you are with your business? Is your pipeline full of leads? Is your business growing on a predictable and consistent basis? If you answered "yes" to all of these questions, then you can stop reading and go back to running your business. Whatever you're doing is working. Most likely, though, you have answered "no" to at least one or more of these questions.

Through my own testing and research, I've found that what used to work in marketing years ago either no longer works at all, or doesn't work as well as it once did. In fact, finding marketing systems that touch the prospect at least three times are needed to acquire a customer. Do you know the value of your ideal customer for the initial transaction, for the year, for the lifetime of the client? If you do not know these numbers, you will not be able to make an educated decision about what you're willing to invest in acquiring a new client.

I also mentioned the term, "ideal customer." Have you identified your ideal customer? You have to get specific for this to be effective. For example, what does your ideal client drive? What clothes do they wear? Do they golf? Do they fish? Do they hunt? Do they boat? Do they play tennis? What do they read? What kind of music do they listen to? What are their hobbies? How much money do they make? What do they spend their money on?

Are you getting the idea? Learn who your true ideal clients are. With the marketing strategies we have available to us today, we can use this type of specific information to reach our target markets directly.

In summary, you need to find out what you're willing to invest into acquiring a new client and who that ideal client truly is. With these two pieces of information, you can develop a marketing plan.

You may not be aware of what kinds of marketing are even available today. Years ago, if you were just listed in the Yellow Pages that was all you needed in order to get the phone to ring. As you know, the overall usage of the Yellow Pages has certainly gone down, but I wouldn't tell you to get out of the Yellow Pages all together. Certain demographics still use the Yellow Pages and with less and less advertisers *in* the Yellow Pages, you have less competition.

Do not to simply list your website address in your Yellow Pages ad. You want to give people a reason to visit your website or pick up the phone and call you. For example, what value could you give away to attract website visitors or generate phone calls? Could it be a free 27-point inspection and analysis (instead of the overused free estimate)? Could it be a free video series they access from your website? Could it be a free coupon or series of coupons they can only obtain by going to your website and entering their contact information? Could it be a download of a consumer report that outlines the top mistakes people make when hiring a XYZ company? And by the way, the report should be about how you do things differently from other companies. These are just a few of the lead generation magnets you should use in your traditional marketing.

If you're using traditional marketing such as the Yellow Pages, radio, TV, newspapers, magazines, and others, you should at least be using lead generation magnets and presenting irresistible offers so they raise their hand to you and say, "Yes! I'm interested in learning more about what you have to offer."

They're looking at your ads that stand out from everybody else's because *your* ads have calls to action. With people exposed to over 5,000 advertising messages on average per day, it takes more "touches" than ever before.

How will your marketing get through the clutter?

Keep in mind that marketing to your existing clients will always be easier than marketing to potential clients. Your existing customers already know you and your company; they already know the level of service you provide, and they already know who you are. Existing clients are going to be the easiest to market and sell to, and I certainly recommend starting with your existing clients in mind.

Additionally, we continue to implement and test multiple campaigns to acquire new customers. These campaigns are based on specific products, and sometimes to specific audiences. For example, we have campaigns dedicated to the dentist niche, offering a reputation marketing product specific to helping dentists. By targeting a specific niche, our conversions increased. To see our dedicated division

focused to the dentist niche, visit:
www.DentistReviewAccelerator.com.

In today's world of marketing, you have to get through the clutter. In fact, in one of our campaigns we actually sent a personalized video book in the mail. The dentist's name was printed on the book and when the dentist opened the book, a personalized video played explaining how we can help the dental practice with their reviews. Since this is such a cutting-edge marketing piece, the video book almost always gets through the clutter, right to the dentist. Then, we follow-up the video book with a CD, Rubik's Cube, and a letter about 10 days later. The message of this campaign is, "I am puzzled you didn't order the Dentist Review Accelerator; maybe you didn't have time to watch the video so I have enclosed an audio CD to play in the car." Then, another 10 days later, we send a trash can in the mail with this message, "Don't throw this opportunity away - Throw away the trash talk with the Dentist Review Accelerator."

The first mail sequence with the video book is sent via FedEx, as FedEx tends to have a higher open rate. The second sequence we send in a clear plastic bag, so they are guaranteed to see the CD and Rubik's Cube. This certainly gets through the clutter, makes the office staff laugh and most often finds its way to the dentist. The final sequence with the trash can also stands out. Our trash can has to be on the top of the pile of mail. It's hard to stack letters on top of our mini-trash can. In short, this is a very involved campaign, but it gets through the clutter and proves a winning ROI for our review system.

In addition to building this direct mail campaign for the dentists, we have also built a dedicated website, wrote a dedicated eBook, and created a dedicated video series. This campaign cost around $115 per prospect, which may initially sound high to you. However, I know what my lifetime value is and I'm willing to spend $115 to acquire one customer. Obviously, I won't gain a new customer for every piece I send out, but through testing, I've been able to determine how many I need to send out in order to acquire one new client. I also know I'll need two new clients to break even in the first year or any dentist that stays on for more than one year, turns this into a profitable campaign.

This video book campaign is obviously on the extreme side, but at a minimum I have found you will need three "touches" via a strategic direct mail campaign in order to get through the clutter. For example, just sending a postcard once with no follow-up piece is no longer as effective as it once was. Postcards are good for the first step as they are inexpensive and if you have the wrong address, you aren't wasting a lot of money finding that out. In terms of postage, I always recommend sending first class to ensure your direct mail gets delivered. Also, if the address is wrong, you will get the piece back in the mail, now knowing the address needs to be corrected. Additionally, I always recommend following up with multiple pieces or "touches" after the postcard.

I share these direct mail strategies with you so you start thinking outside of the box. We talk more about direct mail in chapter eleven. Also, I would recommend planning out a marketing calendar as part of your marketing plan. A marketing calendar makes it easy to view your marketing plan for the next 12 months. A calendar is imperative to using multiple medias in your promotions and tying together the different media to improve the results of your campaigns. For example, being able to strategically plan out a direct mail campaign with email, video, Facebook posts, Twitter, and other media is easy to see and implement with a marketing calendar.

Additionally, by adding a marketing calendar to your marketing plan, you can grow your business strategically and much quicker. A calendar adds accountability to your marketing plan and is available for reference any time you need it. Hang it up on the wall and hold yourself – as well as your employees – accountable for the work that needs to be done to grow your business.

At this point you may be overwhelmed, confused, or even frustrated with the fact that you have to think about these types of strategies and medias in marketing today in order to grow your business. Or maybe you think you have enough information to go and create your own marketing calendar on your own. Great! But for those of you who feel you need a little more help and insight, keep reading. If you still feel as though you could use some professional assistance and guidance once you've read this book, there is help available. I would recommend signing up for our additional resources, which are currently complimentary at www.JimmysGift.com. These resources are an extension of this book and will provide further insight. Also, seek out advice from a marketing consultant or marketing agency.

With that being said, let's backtrack just a little. If you're already in business, you've already named your business and had a logo designed. However, it may be time for a new and updated logo. In the next chapter, I uncover some of the inner workings of building your brand, how that affects your business and marketing, and why maintaining a good reputation is a key element to growing and expanding your business.

Chapter Four
Building Your Brand

Every company needs a brand. These days, even individual people need a brand. If you're an author, for example, you're branding yourself and your author name, be it your own name or a pseudonym. So many people are building a brand online now that it's a little overwhelming to think about on a global scale, but your job is to focus on yourself and your business.

The first thing you need is a business name. When brainstorming a business name, keep in mind that it should be easy to remember and easily associated with whatever products or services your business will provide. This comes partially in time and with proper marketing, too; for example, Apple wouldn't be an obvious choice for branding a computer/tech company, but it works. Apple is well-known and has been around long enough to be associated with computers. The name McDonald's wouldn't be associated with fast food unless they had done a great job of making that happen. Using something more obvious or easily associable is just one way that makes choosing a business name less daunting.

According to naming experts, business names should communicate what your business does while staying open to business expansion. People also prefer real words as opposed to fabricated words, although fabricated or combined words can often have a very positive effect, too. Think of Kodak or Google - these are not real words, but they immediately make you think of specific companies and products. In fact, Google has become so big it has turned into a verb when people need to search online for information. People now typically say, "Google it."

Keeping your name open for future business expansion is another important aspect of naming your business. If you name your business after a region or a specific product, it may be more difficult to expand later on. Amazon is a wonderful example of this: they started as an online bookseller but now are the largest online retailer of almost everything. If they had named their business with books in mind, this expansion may not have been possible.

Your business name should also be available as a domain name, preferably a dot com. This is also a good way to make sure no one already has your business name: Google it. It's also a good way to ensure that your business name is the absolute highest ranking keyword in use so if someone searches for your business name and you own the dot com, it may organically appear at the top of the search list more easily.

Your business name is one way to associate yourself and your brand with what you do. If the original name you had planned is unavailable, do some more brainstorming to determine another name that fits. Ultimately, your brand will be associated with your business name, and your brand includes a number of different things:

- ✧ How you present your business
- ✧ Your website's design and professionalism
- ✧ The level of service associated with your business
- ✧ Your logo and what impression it makes on your audience
- ✧ The main focus of your business and its products and services
- ✧ The level of customer service your business provides
- ✧ The quality of the products your business sells

The list goes on, but these are some of the basics. Your business name is not the be-all and end-all of branding, though it does play an important part. Your brand will ultimately be determined by the inner workings and outer presentation of your business, not just by your name and logo.

Speaking of which... how important is a strong logo for your business? Different businesses use different logo styles and designs to help people recognize their brand without having to use the full company name. Just like your company's name and website, your logo is a way to integrate what your business offers and the level of service it provides with an image or design.

A good logo is easily reproducible, looks good in black and white as well as color, and is recognizable when it's large as well as when it's small. With that in mind, sit down and have a brainstorming session, either by yourself or with a group of people who know about your business idea and what it will offer.

Begin by writing down the main concept of your business. What products or services will your business offer? Who is your target audience? Break down the products and services your business will offer into detailed parts. For example, if you plan to offer marketing services, what kinds of packages will your company offer? How will social media marketing be included? What are some of the main facts you know about various types of marketing?

This will get your mind focused in the right direction to come up with a solid business name and maybe even a logo at the same time. Once you've brainstormed and written down some ideas, look back over your notes to see which names and logos you've come up with that are the most appropriate and the best suited for your business.

After that, I recommend taking a step back and looking over the notes again after a good night's sleep. This will give you a fresh perspective – and you might have more ideas in the meantime.

After you have defined what services/products you will offer, your target audience, and the overall impression you want to give, I recommend having your logo designed via crowdsourcing. If you Google, "logo crowdsourcing," you will see many websites offering this service. By offering a prize of $300 to $1,000, designers from all over the world will submit their logo designs to your contest. The result will be over 50 logos to choose from. The higher the prize value, the more entries you typically receive. You then narrow down the logos to a few and continue to tweak until a winner is selected. The winner gets the prize money and the website providing the service takes their cut. I recommend 99Designs.com and LogoTournament.com.

Logo, colors, and your overall image make up your external brand. However, you should also be aware of your internal brand. This becomes more and more important as you grow and your business becomes larger. Internal branding includes how your employees answer the phone, the processes you have in place, your level of customer service, etc. Everything within a business is marketing. We are always marketing and need to be aware of our internal branding, which in turn helps our external branding.

Chapter Five
Your Website

Today, many people use online search engines such as Google, Yahoo!, Bing, and others to seek out services, products, and businesses from national companies down to local shops. However, some people still use the Yellow Pages or word-of-mouth to find businesses. Whatever method people use to seek out businesses, all methods typically lead to a website. Your website is the foundation to all of your marketing. It needs to be laid out effectively, easy to navigate, consistent with your brand, and built to be search engine friendly so your business shows up higher on search results.

I want to take a step back and ask you a couple of questions. First, why do you want to have a website? Or why do you think you even *need* a website? Is it because you think every business just needs to have a website today? Is it because you want to educate your existing clients on the products and services you offer? Is it to attract new clients? Over the next few days, reflect on how and why a website could be important to your organization.

I find that many small business owners think extremely fast. As a small business owner myself, I have this trait as well, which can usually be very helpful in building your organization at a quicker pace. However, thinking too fast can be a detriment to your overall goals. Take the time to think about what the ultimate goal of having a website is. This is crucial to setting up an effective site.

Ultimately, most business owners want their website to help them obtain more leads, which will then turn into more sales and profits. If that is the case, I want to also ask you if your existing, more traditional marketing is tying in to your website. For example, in your Yellow Page ad, are you just listing your website address? Or is it giving prospects a reason to go to your website for something specific such as a free exclusive video series, a downloadable report, a free gift, or something of value for the prospect in exchange for their contact information?

So, you then have someone that has raised their hand and said, "Hmm, I may be interested in your products and services but I want to learn a little more first." You now have a lead.

Think of how people date. You typically don't ask the other person to marry you on the first date. You need to explore the relationship, build trust, and learn about the other person in order to determine if it is the right match. Well, it's the same in developing marketing systems and lead generation funnels that nurture the prospect into gaining trust and ultimately becoming a client. The next chapter will provide multiple methods to attract people into your lead generation process.

Depending on what systems you have in place for following up with a lead, you can begin to build your relationship with this person and hopefully convert them into a client. Some systems can be automated in terms of building that relationship. In chapter six which is about lead generation magnets, I will discuss Infusionsoft, the system we use which automates our marketing process for leads and even our existing clients.

The first step in developing a lead funnel is a website to capture the prospect's attention and then entice them enough for the prospect to provide their contact information. Keeping in mind that people love free value, let's take a closer look into websites.

There are a number of different kinds of websites, and each business has its own unique needs. These needs will determine the best kind of website for your business and your target audience. Knowing what options are available for you will help you to choose the kind of site best suited for your business. This chapter will provide further details of these options.

Today, having a website is not enough. You want to ensure you are providing your website visitors the best experience with landing page optimization in mind. You want to include calls to action within your website to give visitors a reason to raise their hand and say, "Yes, I am interested, but I may not be ready to buy your product or service today." Even integrating live chat into your website is highly recommended to provide an instant interactive experience. Live chat will be discussed in more detail within the next chapter. In short, automated systems can market to your prospect over time via email, direct mail, or even text messages to help build bonding and rapport, while keeping you in their top-of-mind awareness as your prospect gets closer to their buying decision.

Single Page Websites

This type of website is perfect for a quick splash page for a business or a specific product or service. While this is one page, the site can have links to PDFs and other websites. As a one-page site, high visibility on major search engines will be difficult. Using Google Express may be a cost-effective way to guarantee exposure.

There are definite pros and cons to using a one-page website, but if your product or service is laser-focused, you don't need much more than a single page to showcase your work. For example, certain types of restaurants can easily get away with some pictures and their menu. Regardless of which website style you choose, it's a good idea to have some online presence, such as a single page website, to add credibility.

Simple Websites

A simple website contains roughly five to ten web pages. These pages include the usual global navigation like Home, About, and Contact. The rest of the pages will vary depending on your business, but this is fairly easy to customize if you're using a user-friendly platform or hire a web designer to create it for you. Explore the website for my dedicated web design division, EasyWebCreations.com, where we specialize in building websites that are search engine friendly and help convert website visitors into leads.

A simple website design is perfect for a small business with several products or services available. Your web presence will be easier to establish through search engine optimization and search engine rankings because your site will be larger than a single page website. Also, it is important that your website be built on a platform that makes it easy for you to update your website. The more you update the content on your site, the higher it will typically rank on search engines. We predominantly recommend and use WordPress.

More Customized Websites

If you want a completely unique design and do not want to work from a template, a highly-customized website can be created in a number of different ways. You can hire a professional or go to a website such as 99designs.com, freelancer.com, or designcrowd.com and choose the design bid that best fits your business.

The downfall to using a design bidding site is having to know exactly what you're looking for in terms of search engine optimization, landing pages, and customization. The benefit of crowd sourcing the design is being able to compare a number of design options. Also, once you have the design you will still need to take it to a different person or company to actually convert that design into a WordPress website or whichever platform you choose.

If you choose to have a professional design team create your site, you have the advantage of learning along the way, as well as being able to direct how things will look. You'll also have help with search engine optimization and rankings on the search engines. Obviously, be sure to do your homework on the company you decide to work with. Make sure you feel comfortable working with them. They should be leading you and giving you ideas instead of you dictating what you want. You want to team up with a web design company who are experts because this can be the difference in building a website in which people click the back button and leave your website or a website that engages and ultimately turns visitors into leads.

There's also the option of creating your site completely on your own through a design site such as weebly.com, wix.com, or squarespace.com, all of which will charge you either an annual or monthly fee to host your sites. We have found these sites to be less effective in attracting traffic and actually converting visitors into leads. Mainly because these services tend to be more limiting compared to a simple or customized site that is built by a top web design company.

Using Squeeze Pages and Landing Pages

A squeeze or landing page's purpose is to intrigue the

prospective customer enough for them to want more information so they enter their email address to receive more. Capturing a prospective client's email address is almost mandatory in order to make a sale or gain a client these days. Once you capture their email address you can then market to them over time. People are exposed to so many marketing and advertising elements every day; it takes multiple "touches" before the customer is actually ready to purchase. If the prospect does not, the prospect simply does not trust you yet. You will want to have your lead generation funnel continue to warm up the prospect, continue to build credibility and this ultimately will lead to a conversion.

By utilizing a landing page, you'll be able to capture email addresses and add them to your email list without an issue. This will allow you to send follow-up emails, automate a series of emails to be sent out, and ultimately have your potential customer get to know you and your business and make that first purchase.

Typically, you'll want to test multiple landing pages to see which ones convert more. For example, you can have Google Adwords split test traffic to two or more different landing pages. This will allow you to see which pages lead to more opt-ins and conversions.

Membership Portal Websites

Membership websites are ideal for people in fields such as coaching or other teaching careers. A membership site can also be helpful to those who want to share their knowledge and expertise with others in their field. With a membership portal site, you can offer your training materials to others in your field without making these materials available for the whole Internet to see. For example, a local builder could have a membership site sharing his/her best strategies that he/she markets to other builders throughout the world. Or a fitness instructor could have a membership site share their best strategies to lose weight, allowing them to help more people throughout the world. Inside the membership site can be downloadable PDFs, videos, reports, forums for the community to interact with one another, and more.

You can choose to have visitors pay to join your membership site or give them access for free. The decision to charge visitors or provide free information will depend on your business model and goals.

Additionally, it is imperative to have some sort of "deliverable" when people register such as a DVD, binder, audio CD, or book. This helps lower your return rates. You can choose to have customers pay monthly or one-time for a package, or both. A live event can also help with keeping your refund rates low.

These websites are perfect for starting an information marketing business. For example, if you want to teach other business owners throughout the world the techniques and strategies you have mastered over time, this membership site can accomplish this. This will allow you to share your knowledge with other people in your industry, outside of your immediate area. You can start leveraging your time and stop trading hours for dollars.

Mobile Websites

A mobile website is a mini version of your website that loads automatically if a visitor is viewing your website on their mobile phone. If the visitor is viewing your website on their iPad, tablet, or computer, your full version website will load. This is for the business owner or organization who wants to capitalize on increasing mobile traffic. Internet usage on mobile phones is soaring.

Having a mobile version of your website helps increase visibility on both mobile search and traditional search. For search engines, having a mobile device is an easy differentiator. For example, Google typically ranks a website higher if it has a dedicated mobile version.

To be able to have a mobile site, you would either hire a professional or use a mobile website builder online if you prefer to do it yourself. It is recommended to hire a professional if you don't have experience coding or if you just simply don't have time to learn another new skill to make your business more widely available.

Updating Your Website

Your website should be updated on a consistent basis. The more you update your website, typically the higher your search engine ranking will be. Additionally, having a professional-looking website that is updated on a regular basis will lead to more sales and conversions. Regularly updated sites also have more credibility than sites that tend to sit for months or years at a time.

Your website is a 24-hour communicator to your prospective clients and existing customers. If they need a piece of information, it should be easy to find on your website. However, when a site hasn't been updated for six months or longer, a customer tends to stop taking it seriously and wonders if the information they're getting is the best they have access to.

This is another reason why you should want to keep your site updated on a consistent basis and make sure all the information is current. Keeping your site updated also raises your search engine rankings, making your site and your business more visible to new customers.

There are professionals who can also provide these services for you, or if your website is built in an easy to use platform such as WordPress, you can update your website easily yourself. From websites to social media, these professionals can make sure your updates are worded properly, stay professional, and are designed to promote your company in a valuable way.

Checking and Monitoring Your Website

The Internet changes all the time. When was the last time you looked at your website on a PC, laptop, iPad, iPad Mini, mobile phone, and a Mac? Ensuring your website looks great on all of these devices is part of the process of website usability analysis, along with making sure your site functions the same and is visible across multiple browsers such as Google Chrome, Firefox, Internet Explorer, Opera, and Safari.

I recommend having your web design company check your site on multiple platforms at least quarterly as browsers change constantly. This will ensure your website continues to look great on all devices and also will help maximize your visibility. Browsers change and, often times, an older website will not look as good as it once did. Macs have different fonts than PCs, so it is important that your website is checked on both PC and Mac.

Along with this conundrum also comes the process of tracking your traffic, what keywords people are using to find your site, and continually checking up on your traffic and what content is the most popular. Google Analytics provides a free method to track this data.

Again, there are several ways to do this and to make sure that you're getting the most from your web traffic. You can try to learn how to do this yourself by researching online or investing in some professional training. The other option is to hire a professional to help you analyze your site and show you how to do so in the process. In fact, I recommend, having a professional look at this data on a monthly basis at a minimum. A professional can quickly look at your data and make recommendations to improve your visitor experience, increase the time your visitors spend on your website, and help increase the conversion of website visitors into actual leads.

The Use of Multiple Websites

I have found conversions to be the most effective when creating multiple sites directed to specific niches. To increase your sales and conversion, consider building mini-sites to specific niches.

For example, on www.JimmyMarketing.com we offer Reputation Marketing services to all small businesses. However, we identified dentists as a particular niche in which our review system works extremely well. Rather than refer the dentists to a page within Jimmy Marketing, we built an entire website dedicated to dentists which you can visit at www.DentistReviewAccelerator.com. By having this dedicated website, this has allowed us to serve more dentists throughout the United States.

Chapter Six
Lead Generation Magnets

Lead generation magnets will generate more leads for your business. Your website visitors must be enticed to provide their contact information. If you use multiple lead generation magnets, you can bundle them into a lead generation "downloadable kit" which has the most perceived value to a website visitor based on a survey conducted by Ryan Deiss, who is the industry's leading expert on traffic conversion.

Think about how much more valuable a "downloadable kit" sounds compared to a simple PDF download. Ryan's obvious tip: "Don't try to reinvent the wheel too much here. If you want to gather business leads, then offer what's most valuable. Make it simple and easy for the customer to get value from you!" I recommend taking it a step further and dropping "downloadable." Go with a kit in which you use direct mail to mail your prospect a book, an audio CD, a DVD, etc. Sending something in the mail allows you to connect to your prospect easier than sending an email to your prospect. Overall, we are finding great success with direct mail.

Giving away informational products of value or a product sample pack for free is usually the way to go when you're requesting a prospect's contact information. The best part of all this is you only put in the time to create these products once and you can use them over and over again. There are a number of different things you can give away for free to make sure your potential client or customer receives something of value. Let's go over these in more detail.

Video Series

A free video series is an excellent way to give your potential customers more information and educate them on some of the things you offer. People love videos because it doesn't strain the eyes like reading pages and pages of text on a screen, they can multi-task while they're watching, which saves them time and makes things more convenient, and it's just easier to watch a video and take notes than it is to read a screen and take notes. Think about it: you pause, write something down and then have to find your spot again. With a video, you can write while the video continues to play or simply push the pause button and continue after you take some notes.

Video is also great because it helps you leverage your time. You can create a video once and use it over and over again for each new potential client. You can choose to speak directly to your audience without necessarily investing time into a call or chat session every time. Depending on your business, you can use this platform to introduce your products and services, educate your audience about industry basics, or simply introduce yourself in the first video.

Not only is this a time-saver, but it also gives you a face and a voice for your audience and makes you more approachable. Not that you can't communicate being approachable in writing; a video is just that much more effective as far as your likability is concerned. When people like you, they're more likely to pay attention to you and follow your activities. Most importantly, they are more likely to trust you, and when they trust you, they will buy from you. That means a larger audience, more prospective clients, and an impression of sincerity for your audience. If you haven't boarded the video train yet for your website and business, then you're definitely missing out! I'll be going into more detail about how effective video is and how you can create your own videos in chapter seven.

Email Series

Ah, the e-newsletter. People all over the world send and receive newsletters on a daily basis to educate, to inform, to share, to sell, or to promote offers or new products and services. The good part? People can read the email when they have the time, making it accessible to everyone and easy to access whenever (or wherever these days with mobile web access). The bad part? There are so many!

With all the clutter out there, it's essential to create an email series that is thought-provoking, provides value, and gives back to your audience and potential clients. The good news is that you only have to create this email series once if you're utilizing an automated marketing tool, such as Infusionsoft to streamline this process.

This means you can sit down and develop a comprehensive, detailed, and genuinely informative email campaign *once* and have it sent out to each and every potential prospect or client on a predetermined schedule, automatically. That's pretty amazing!

To get through the clutter of emails people tend to receive, it's important to create intriguing subject lines that make people want to open the email, with content that teaches, inspires, and educates people. Of course, you can do all sorts of things with content, too. You can include links, images, text in various colors and sizes, and whatever else you can think of to include.

There are a number of platforms available, including free

ones if you're just getting started. Infusionsoft is the best option if you're further along in your business, but there are also services available for free such as MailChimp. This platform is user-friendly, allowing you to add prospects to your email list automatically by utilizing the form builder to create a form. I have also used Constant Contact which has some functionality built-in for an automated follow-up sequence. Constant Contact is a great starting point because of its low price point, with great functionality.

To create a valuable email series, you should somehow link all of your emails with similar topics or educational materials. If they like the first email, they're more likely to pay attention to the second; if they like the second, they're more likely to pay attention to the third, and so on. Consider all of this while you're creating your various emails as a whole and individually. Most of all, remember the golden rule: provide value.

Coupon Download

Everyone loves saving money! Coupons for a certain amount off a product or a discount on services are a great way to generate interest, earn trust, and give the customer incentive to share their email address with you on your website. Depending on your business, you can offer coupons for a limited time, coupons for an extended amount of time, coupons for a product, coupons for a service, coupons for a book or other educational product, and the list goes on. You also don't have to necessarily call them coupons; you can call them gift certificates, discount codes, or come up with your own spin on words that fit your business (think "Burger Bucks" by Burger King).

Of course, what your coupons are for and how much your customer gets discounted is up to you. We're all in business to make a profit, but that doesn't mean you can't give fairly steep discounts to incredibly valuable prospects and clients.

Another option is to offer additional incentives for customers to purchase a product or service with you, like a gift card or cash prize.

EBooks

Another great way to capture a customer's interest is by offering a free eBook in exchange for their email information. They can be written and created based on what you know about your field and what you can teach others. Usually, free eBooks are given away in PDF format, but you may choose to go a step further and give your audience an option to choose between a PDF version and a Kindle or Nook version.

I know quite a bit goes into creating an eBook – it has to be written, edited, and converted; not to mention, you need a design for the cover created. It almost seems a shame to give it away for free, doesn't it? But if you determine your potential customers' value versus the cost of creating an eBook once, and consider that you can use it over and over again to gain clients, you'll see that the cost of creating the eBook will be earned back in the form of valuable clients.

So how do you go about creating an eBook? Well, the first thing you need to do is write it. If you can't find the time to write it, you can seek out a ghostwriter who has experience or interest in what you do in your business. Most people have never hired a ghostwriter, so here are some basics.

Where to find a ghostwriter:

✧ oDesk.com

- ✧ Elance.com
- ✧ Freelancer.com
- ✧ Guru.com

These are the top freelance websites online today. Many of them have been around for a number of years, and all have writers for hire who you can check out by looking at their profiles and portfolios. The site you choose is up to you. I recommend oDesk.com. They are well-known all over the world and charge the least for their services; their site is also easy to use, and there are a number of talented ghostwriters and general writers available.

What to look for in a writer:

- ✧ Experience – My recommendation is that the writer has at the very least five years of experience writing, preferably in a number of different styles. Five years of professional experience is a good amount of time for the writer to learn enough to adapt to multiple genres or styles, but 10 years is the best – a writer is constantly honing their skills to be better, and those without a formal writing-oriented education gain their education through real life experience.
- ✧ Variety in their experience – If you want to create an eBook focusing on business, make sure the writer has some nonfiction writing experience, such as eBooks, articles, and other business-oriented materials like white papers or reports. Though a writer may be talented, someone who writes short fiction isn't necessarily the best fit for a business-related eBook.
- ✧ Professionalism – The writer must look good on paper (or on screen, in the case of telecommuters), but that's almost a given when looking for a writer. I recommend speaking to the potential writer via phone or Skype to get to know who they are and see if you mesh well

together. If the writer has spelling errors or grammatical discrepancies in their portfolio or on their website, they probably aren't the best choice.

✧ Availability – If you get in touch with a potential writer and interview them for your book project, they should be available through multiple channels (Skype, text/cell, email, and the freelance site itself; potentially even Facebook) and any request or question sent out during the week should be answered within two days, three at the most.

✧ Excellent spelling and grammar – Unless you're open to hiring an editor separately from a writer, you can hire a writer without flawless English skills. However, to save an additional step and money, find a writer who knows how to self-edit after the first draft.

Once you have a writer and the book is ready to go, it's time to make a choice: should this eBook be available strictly as a PDF file? Or should this eBook also be made available for eBook reading devices?

When considering this choice, there are a few things to keep in mind. PDF files are easy to create. You can keep it very simple by using Word or another word processor to create the eBook, even adding borders and line breaks, and then converting that to a PDF file using Word. A properly formatted eBook for the Kindle and Nook is a little more complicated. Sure, you can go through Kindle Direct Publishing and simply upload a Word file. However, because eReading devices read HTML source files, the formatting will often appear inconsistent, off, or have a lot of blank screens when readers turn the page. This means finding someone who can hand-code the source file and make sure the book's presentation is professional. You can go and find a freelancer through the sites listed above that can complete these tasks.

You can also learn to do it yourself if you have HTML experience. The best book to walk you through the process is called *Kindle Formatting: The Complete Guide* by Joshua Tallent. It's still a good idea to test the file on an actual Kindle device before publishing it and sending it out into the world. You'll be able to find glitches and issues that other ways of testing will not find. This is similar to usability testing for websites, only specifically for eBooks.

A Published Book

Having your own book published certainly positions you as an expert authority in your niche. You can use the same concepts and strategies previously discussed as an eBook, but actually get your book published. One of the biggest advantages of a print book over an eBook is the ability to ship your book to your prospect. For some, you may be thinking, "Oh no, more money." To the smarter marketer, it is clear that you now have your prospect's mailing address and you can now continue to market using direct mail which has a higher conversion ratio than email marketing.

If you don't want to go through the painstaking steps of submitting your manuscript to traditional publishers, then the best way of getting a book published in print is to self-publish it. If you're working with a trade paperback, your best bet is to use the print on demand platform, CreateSpace (CS). CS is an Amazon company and your book can even be listed as published under your own press, which can be named as a derivative of your business.

The main things you need for a self-published book are the content, a book cover, an International Standard Book Number (ISBN), and an expanded distribution package through your CS account. For the best possible presentation, you want to use Word and re-size your pages to 6" x 9". Once you've done this, you can upload the content file to CS and they will do an automated print check. When working on your book's cover, you can either use the cover builder on the CS website or create your own by using Photoshop or another image editing software. If your content pages are 6" x 9", you can calculate your book's cover size fairly easily as well. The cover is usually uploaded as a one-piece PDF file. In other words, your cover should take the back cover, spine, and front cover into consideration, along with a bit of extra space around the edges called "bleed."

Again, you can hire a freelancer to do this for you or you can use the crowdsourcing sites mentioned previously. Then, you again upload the file and CS will do an automated print check to let you know if any adjustments need to be made.

Purchasing an ISBN and expanded distribution can be done directly through your CS account during the upload and publishing process. Currently, CS offers ISBNs for much less than the official source, Bowker. When you purchase your ISBN through CS, you'll be asked to create a Bowker account through the site and will enter information for said account. This is also where you'll enter your press or publishing company name so it appears in the book's metadata. This helps maintain credibility because CS won't be listed as the publisher.

This is a process and does require some know-how, so if it sounds overwhelming or you simply don't have the time for it, hiring a professional will be your best bet. Again, you can use a freelance site such as oDesk.com to find someone you can work with who has experience in the self-publishing field. You want to find someone who has started their own book publishing company or has guided other authors in their self-publishing ventures.

Live Webinars and Seminars

Live webinars and seminars are a cost-effective and efficient way to teach and share valuable information with groups of people. You can even give them the option to simply watch the recorded webinar later if the time scheduled isn't an option for them. If you are having an in-person seminar, you can record the seminar and then send the replay to your attendees or people that missed the seminar.

Webinars are also a good way to practice public speaking. You are not actually in front of a room full of people, but honing your abilities by creating webinars or videos will help you develop your speaking skills in general. Once you do that, you can begin speaking to live audiences at seminars and conferences without getting as nervous as you would if you hadn't practiced with a virtual audience.

So how do you go about creating a live webinar? The first order of business is to figure out what you want your webinar to focus on. Choose an area of knowledge or business expertise and make a list of smaller tasks you could focus on and talk about during this webinar. Keep in mind that people don't want to waste their time, so they need to learn and they need to stay interested.

A good way to plan out your webinar is to create a list of talking points you'd like to cover and how much time you want to spend on each one. You can then determine sub-points for each topic and go into as much detail as is necessary to teach your audience about that particular task or skill.

Once you've determined your topics and talking points, you'll want to make sure that you've put together some form of visual aid for each of these. One of the best ways to do this is by creating a PowerPoint presentation with slides for each talking point. Keep in mind, when preparing your PowerPoint, use pictures as trigger points for you to talk about certain topics. Do not fill your slides with a bunch of text and then just read from the text. The visual aids should support what you are saying.

When preparing your webinar, you can begin marketing, planning, and scheduling everything. There are a number of services out there that allow you to present to a number of people. These services include GoToMeeting.com, GoToWebinar.com, AnyMeeting.com, OnWebinar.com, and MeetingBurner.com. Many of these offer free trials or a free account, so if you're just getting started and need a viable way to expand, this is a great way to do it.

Seminars are identical in principle with the exception being a live audience rather than video. Make sure you have visual aids, talking points, and remember not to get nervous!

The Evergreen Webinar

This type of webinar is unique because it doesn't rely on dates or changing technology to be successful. The information contained in this specific kind of webinar is evergreen, meaning it will be useful for years to come. That means you can use the recorded version of this webinar as a video on your site, effectively leveraging your time.

An evergreen webinar is all about the content. It has to be written in a way that remains useful and contains relevant information that will be useful for years to come.

Depending on your business or area of expertise, this could be a webinar about a basic aspect of your business that isn't likely to change very soon. Obviously, technology changes all the time and with it so does business, but get back to the essentials, the foundation for your business. That's where the brainstorming for your evergreen webinar should come from.

Article Downloads

Articles are a great way to publish your work, teach your audience, and provide more content online. This helps your audience get to know you, raises your search engine ranking, and you can try to have your work featured as a "Kindle Single" on Amazon (approval required on a per-piece basis).

By writing articles instead of just keeping a blog, you also raise your credibility. People tend to look at an article as more professional than a blog. Anyone can blog. It takes a little more skill to write a quality article.

Whatever your business or field of expertise, you can take smaller chunks out of the big picture and teach people individual processes through articles. These articles can be sent out as an exclusive set of tutorials or as a supplement to a video series. The possibilities are endless – it's your creation! Why not do something a little different? Think of the time you invest as sweat equity into your business. It can only grow from there. If you can make these articles evergreen, too, then you're really on to something.

When you write articles, make sure they're well-researched; cite your source if you quote anything, and make sure your content is different and unique to you and your business. Titles that work really well are usually how-to titles or "5

Secrets to _____ ” and fill in the blank with your topic. Step-by-step articles are good, too, and they help you break everything down into manageable chunks for you, the writer, as well as the reader.

CD / DVD Production

DVDs containing your videos, webinars, or presentations are another great way to connect with your audience and teach them. If you're working on a budget, you can use a program like Jing to do screen capture videos of five minutes or less. You can also record yourself with your webcam with this software. Working on a tight budget means you have to do a lot of things yourself, which isn't necessarily a bad thing, but when it comes to videos and video editing, you'll need to take some time to get to know your software so you can create professional videos.

I'll explain more about videos and how to create them in the next chapter. For now, I want you to know how video can help you with obtaining and sustaining more clients.

Sure, people still read online. But there are so many ways to create videos now that just about everyone can do it. Whether it is a fun project, a business project, or just a video to say hello, there are a number of free programs available now that will let you create videos of your own and post them online.

The reason people love videos is because they're almost effortless to watch. You can watch one on your lunch break, too, which is an added bonus for people at work on a mobile device. People can take notes if they want to, pause without needing to find the spot where they left off, and no one has to deal with bad spelling or grammar.

Now, if you can create a professional series of videos that will also teach your audience something or answer their questions, you'll be able to create a DVD with those videos. Most video editing software will let you splice clips together, create transitions from one video clip to the next, and even input credits and opening title screens.

There are free video editors out there as well as free DVD menu creation software; it's just a matter of finding it and using it for your business.

If you aren't ready for video, or even as a supplement to a DVD, a CD is a great way to get your message out. Also, since you have to mail either a CD or DVD, you will then be able to request the mailing address of your prospect. Direct mail will help you nurture prospects more easily and help convert them into clients faster.

Live Chat

One of the easiest ways to convert visitors into leads is to offer live chat on your website. I highly recommend teaming up with a company that you can outsource your chat to 24/7. Some chat companies will even charge you for the leads that they bring to you. This pay for performance model keeps your initial costs extremely low, and if you are bringing leads into your website via chat, you will be happy to pay the chat company.

If you are only offering live chat during normal business hours, you are missing out on 67% of possible conversions. Even if you have a 24/7 staff, I would still team up with a company that specializes in chat and can bring you highly qualified leads. Then, your staff can be following up with warm leads.

In fact, we have found that one out of every three people that chat with us on our website will eventually do business with us.

Using All of the Above to Create Your Kit

Now that we've covered the different types of lead generation magnets you can utilize, I'll let you in on a little secret:

A number of these can be automated so you don't have to do the work for each and every new potential client.

There are a number of programs out there that allow you to pre-schedule each individual client's follow-up activities ahead of time. The one that I recommend for all of your marketing needs is Infusionsoft. Their service allows you to automate emails, videos, pre-recorded phone calls, and follow-up emails; the possibilities are endless. Your time won't be spent on trying to follow-up manually.

Also, you can automate a good portion of sending out your kit, should you choose to create one with some or all of these materials included. It will definitely take time, effort, and hard work to get the initial kit put together, but once you've finished it and the materials are available, anything that can be sent out via email can be automated; recorded phone calls can be automated; sending snail mail can be automated; and the process of creating and scheduling your webinars can be simplified while also allowing you to send notifications to your email list.

Creating some of these materials is absolutely imperative to growing your business and your audience. Who doesn't want free stuff that will help them? The simple truth is people love free stuff; those who stay on your list and begin participating are the people who are truly interested in what you have to offer. Why not try to create a video right now? Or at least brainstorm what you could talk about to turn it into a video series. What are you waiting for? The opportunities are right at your fingertips. Go seize them!

Chapter Seven
Utilizing Online Video

Video is becoming a vital part of the online experience, and for good reason. What's more incredible than being able to click a button and watch a video? Short videos are usually preferred in order to keep your audience's interest, but longer videos are also acceptable for people who have been following you and already see what you have to offer as well as for topics that need more time for explanation.

One of the main reasons videos are so important is because a video combines your face, the way you move and speak, and the words you're saying. It is the closest thing to seeing someone in person that people can get, besides live video chat. Obviously you won't be online or available 24/7 to live chat with your potential clients and followers.... Having a video on your site just to say hi and offering valuable information is the next best option. Actually, it's better because your time and energy is only required once.

Before I continue, let's just take a quick look at some of the main benefits of using video on your website and in your marketing endeavors.

✧   Oh look! A real person. You know how people are always calling customer service and complaining that there's just a recording on the line with a bunch of options, in some cases never leading to a human who can help you? Annoying, right? Well, right off the bat if you have videos on your site introducing yourself and your business as well as what you offer, it cuts through a lot of the anxiety people feel when being introduced to a new business.

✧   People are people, and even in traditional B2B

companies you're still communicating and selling to or buying from people. If the right people see what you have going on and love it, they'll want to work with you. Video is a great way to do that! Videos give your audience a glimpse into who you are, how you carry yourself, how well-spoken you are, and so on. It's a great way to introduce yourself and share your knowledge while winning someone over. Plus you can use the same videos over and over again, which leverages your time.

✧ Video is available 24 hours a day, 7 days a week, 365 days a year, unless you remove them from your website. If you post a video about a specific product or service you offer, it can act as a sales person for you no matter what you're doing at the same time the potential client is watching. That's pretty amazing!

✧ Video messages leverage your time for the simple reason that they work over and over again, and they do much of the work for you while you're doing something else. From familiarizing your audience with what you do to acting as a sales entity; having videos on your site can save you a great deal of time in the long run.

So how do you go about creating these helpful tools without audio-visual experience? You can do it the hard way and try to learn how to record, edit, and finalize your own videos. The quality may not be fantastic and neither may the presentation, but it's better than not having any videos if you can manage to turn something casual into a more professional presentation. There are a number of free resources, but your best bet is to do some research on video editing software and screen capture software to see which one would be the best for you and your needs. As you grow, you can invest in a professional production team or even build your own in-house team. Bottom line, start creating videos!

The other option is to pay a team of professionals for their skills and get a high quality product that will *definitely* work for you and your business. There are reasonably priced options available. We'll use these as an example for the purpose of this chapter so you know what you can expect to pay, though I do have to say a lot of people would typically charge a lot more than we do. For more detailed information on our pricing, please visit www.JimmyMarketing.com or request our catalog.

Online video is one of the easiest ways to help your visitors feel more comfortable and help convert visitors into prospects and prospects into customers. Our video studio in our Waterford, Connecticut location is equipped with a green screen, which allows us to swap out any background and/or create a custom background. Also, we have a glass teleprompter that reflects the words on glass, so you can look directly into the camera as you use the teleprompter. The videographer adjusts the speed of the teleprompter based on your natural pace so it doesn't sound as if you are reading a script.

I want to briefly go over some types of videos you can produce. I am putting the packages we offer in parentheses so you can then go on our website, www.JimmyMarketing.com to see some specific examples. This way, even if you choose to learn and do this yourself, you'll get a good idea of what kinds of videos convert and bring in more clients and customers.

Slideshow Video (Bronze Video Package)

This is a relatively simple video that will improve your overall visibility on search engines. In fact, Google now displays video results in their search results. This is for the business owner or organization who wants a professional video of pictures and possible narration without being physically visible in the video. I recommend including basic contact information within the video.

Green Screen Video (Silver Video Package)

This type of video provides a professional presentation that can be used on your website and/or on YouTube. You use a green screen in the background and then use software to key-out the green and replace it with any background you choose.

This is for the business owner or organization who wants a professional video with them physically in it with some basic text and basic sound, on their website.

Green Screen Video with Animation (Gold Video Package)

This type of video is very similar to green screen video, but it includes some basic animation. The basic animations are text to help engage the viewer and increase conversions. People stay more engaged when text emphasizes what the person is saying.

Cartooning

This type of video actually draws out a cartoon representing the script that is being narrated. This can now be done digitally, but still giving the look of an artist drawing out the cartoon by hand. This type of video can sometimes convert more than even traditional video. Cartoons are perfect for simplifying more complex processes.

Animation (Custom Package – Animation)

This type of video is similar to cartooning, but it's digital and doesn't look like a drawing. If your video includes animated text, you engage your audience longer while improving their overall impression of the video.

Webcast

A live webcast allows you to stream your video live over the Internet. The audience is able to ask questions via chat as well, and your interaction with your audience is highly professional. This live streaming is like watching TV live, but over the Internet. A free version to use for live streaming is Google Hangout, which will stream you live directly on YouTube via your webcam. Then, the replay becomes available immediately after on YouTube.

Video Series

A video series allows you to educate the visitor over a period of time. The key is for your content to be enticing enough for the visitor to enter their first name and email address for access. A system will then send a series of videos over a number of days. This process builds bonding and rapport and helps the prospect feel more comfortable, which generally results in higher conversions from prospect to client. Again, we highly recommend using an automated marketing solution such as Infusionsoft to accomplish this easily.

Summary

Overall, video helps build bonding and rapport without having to physically talk to each prospect until they are ready to buy. Most importantly, this helps build your email list.

You can use video on your site, in emails, in a physical kit on a DVD, and for a number of mobile devices. Now it's just a matter of getting it done!

Video is one of the best ways to gain your audience's trust and allow them to get to know you. Once your clients trust you and are ready to buy, they'll feel like they know you in person... or pretty close, anyway. In short, video ultimately leads to quicker and more frequent sales.

Chapter Eight
Reputation Marketing

Most marketers refer to this as reputation management. However, you need to build your five star reputation and then effectively market that reputation. Your reputation is one of your most important assets. As prospective clients seek out peer recommendations and reviews about your business, what do they see? Are there reviews posted about your business? Are they good? Reputation marketing helps ensure your online reputation is as strong as it can be.

Reputation marketing is more important than ever. More people go online to review and read reviews about companies and products before they buy almost anything. For authors, Amazon and Goodreads reviews can make or break their book's success rate. For businesses, customer reviews on Yelp, Google, Yahoo, Angie's List, and other review sites for businesses can also make or break their reputation.

Even if you buy other products from Amazon or Ebay, it's common for customers to search similar products if the original product they looked for has bad reviews. Similarly, people are more likely to purchase products from sellers with a high rating as opposed to sellers with a mediocre or low rating.

Would you buy a product or service that has bad ratings and reviews? We've all gone online; we've all looked at hotels, restaurants, reviews of movies, or maybe bought a product on Amazon, and looked at the ratings. If there are bad reviews, are you typically going to buy right away or even buy at all? Of course not, at least not without further research! Looking at reviews is an important factor in decision-making, as you see how other people experience that product or service.

Let's look at another example. There are two dental practices, which are identical. One has 10 good reviews the other has 3 good reviews and 1 bad review. Which dentist office would you visit? Again, they are identical, other than the difference in their online reputation. You would go to the practice with the 10 good reviews. And that's important to know, as you need the foundation of a solid reputation to help increase sales.

According to Nielsen's most recent Global Trust in Advertising study, a whopping 70% of consumers globally reported they trust online reviews from strangers when making their purchasing decisions. Additionally, four out of five consumers say they reversed their purchase decisions based on negative online reviews, according to a Cone study of online trends. To compound the issue, consider that many of your other marketing efforts such as your Yellow Pages ad, social media, direct mail, email, print advertising, PR, and even word-of-mouth referrals are ultimately designed to drive prospective patients to your website. If your reputation is poor or nonexistent, you're likely to lose these prospects to competitors with more savvy online skills. It's clear why online reputation marketing is imperative to your business right now.

Imagine this horrifying scenario: You've been delivering top quality products and/or services consistently for years, exceeding your customers' every expectation. Unbeknownst to you, a former customer posts unfair reviews of your business online – creating a twisted sense of reality. Because you're most likely not encouraging your current clients to post positive reviews, all prospective clients see are these negative comments, resulting in a significant loss of business. Bottom line is if you don't have a system in place to solicit more positive reviews online and you're not monitoring your brand's online reputation, a few negative reviews could ruin your business.

You know your reputation is everything and your most important asset. There is nothing more important than your reputation, as you will see. Additionally, the online marketing game has recently changed. And the good news, your competition doesn't even know about it – yet. So, let's talk about the big game changers that have recently occurred.

Currently, when you put in any business name plus their city in a Google search, Google now reveals the business's reputation. Just recently, Google has merged what is called their Google+ local listing with your business website listing. So, every time you type in any business name (more importantly when you type in your own business name) and your city, it reveals your online reputation.

Moreover, the reviews absolutely end up being perceived as truth when your prospects read the reviews online. Google is also integrating reviews about your business on other review websites into their search results. For example, Google will show Yelp, Citysearch, and other review website ratings within their own search results.

Every type of marketing, especially online marketing, is impacted by your reputation. Google is now showing ratings within the Google Map, Google+ Local, and even pay-per-click (PPC) listings. Not having a reputation or having a poor reputation can have a direct impact on conversions.

I don't need to tell you that it's the information age. What I do want to reiterate is that online reviews are extremely important and can easily influence a potential customer's buying decision. According to another study done by Cone, Inc., 89% of consumers will trust online reviews. Furthermore, 80% have changed their mind about a purchase based on negative feedback. That's a lot! Additionally, 87% stated their decision to purchase was reinforced by positive reviews. On top of all of this, 85% of consumers research products online before they buy, and the same percentage are more likely to purchase a product or service if they read online recommendations or positive reviews.

(For a full article on online reviews and the source of these statistics, please go to: www.fortune3.com/blog/2011/08/statistics-on-ecommerce-and-customer-reviews-online/.)

Reviews can also send you prequalified, presold customers because prospective customers trust reviews as much as personal recommendations. Now if I were to ask any business owner, "Would you rather build a business with customers that don't know you, don't like you, or don't trust you or a referral business where people know you, like you, and trust you?" Hence, everyone would answer (and I'm sure you would, too), "a referral business." With reputation marketing you can build a referral business to brand new prospective customers that have never even been to your business, because consumers trust reviews as much as personal recommendations.

Based on a recent study we completed, 72% of consumers trust reviews as much as personal recommendations. When you have a five star reputation and have these reviews on your website, you have reviews online that are just as much an influence as someone's mother saying, "Yes, you should definitely go to XYZ Dental office," or, "Yes, I go to XYZ Dental Office and it is always a great experience." So, look at it this way, three out of four consumers trust online reviews just as much as personal recommendations. Let me give you an even bigger example of this. Remember what I shared earlier – Nielsen's most recent Global Trust in Advertising study – a whopping 70% of consumers globally report trusting online reviews from strangers when making purchasing decisions. Both our study and Nielsen's study revealed three out of four consumers trust online reviews when making their buying decision.

Managing reviews can be a full-time job in and of itself, depending on your business. That's why businesses specializing in reputation management and reputation marketing are sprouting up all over the country.

Obviously, you can't market a reputation if you have no reviews. So the first step is to go out and get some! Ask your clients for reviews and testimonials. The more people you work with, the more will likely send you positive feedback (if you're doing a good job). So work hard, do a good job, and ask your clients for reviews! Most will say, "I'd be happy to send you a testimonial!"

The more of these you can get and post on your website, the better. Once you've established yourself, you can start asking clients to post their feedback on sites like Yelp and Google+ Local. This will increase your online visibility and reviews should hopefully have high ratings, at least four stars.

When you start receiving reviews on these sites, it's important to monitor what's occurring in your business so you can correct any mistakes and approach any customer who has had a bad experience and provide a solution. This is part of reputation marketing. Your company's success is largely based on its reputation, and the better its reputation, the more business you'll bring in. That's the whole point, right?

Having positive reviews online and asking for feedback will help you to continue to build a better relationship with customers. Additionally, having positive reviews displayed publicly on review websites helps build credibility and increase visibility.

By asking for feedback from your clients, you improve customer service, strengthen your relationship with your clients, and improve your staff and your team. Having a strong, positive reputation will help convert prospects into clients. Additionally, the better the reviews and the more of them posted online, the higher your ranking on the search engines.

Last but not least, I'd like to say that a bad review isn't necessarily the end of the world, nor are reviews 100% accurate. Companies hire people to post fake reviews all the time; although difficult to spot at times, you can usually tell whether a review is real or not. But, regardless of whether a review is real or fake, it still affects your online reputation. If a company is caught leaving fake reviews, it could harm their business a lot more than a couple of bad reviews can. After all... no one likes to do business with a dishonest company.

I believe reputation marketing to be an extremely important part of running a successful business; therefore, I have built an entire division within my company that focuses on reputation marketing. In fact, we even have a reputation product I developed to help businesses get more positive reviews published online from clients, automatically. You can learn more about this product, by visiting www.JimmyMarketing.com and clicking on Reputation Marketing under Services. You can also see our version that has been tailored for dental offices at www.DentistReviewAccelerator.com.

Reputation marketing can help you take your business to great levels. If you don't manage your online reviews and reach out to consumers who left negative ones, there's a good chance that your business won't grow at all... it may even fail due to these online reviews. So, why not make sure you address the problem if it arises, or take preventative measures before it has a chance to arise? That makes good business sense.

Chapter Nine
Traffic Generation

We covered lead generation magnets in chapter six and now, within this chapter, I'll go over how this can help get more traffic to your site, improve your search engine rankings, and how the use of directory submissions can help you achieve these goals.

Having a website is meaningless if you aren't attracting visitors. Some businesses do not require traffic generation because they use their website as a tool with their existing clients. If you are not using your website as a marketing tool to your existing clients, be sure to save room in the budget for traffic generation of new prospects.

Pretty much everyone has *heard* of traffic generation, but how do you go about getting more people to visit your website? There are a number of ways to go about this, and the best way is to use a combination of all of these techniques to get your site the most exposure. Let's take a closer look at some of the ways you can generate more traffic.

Keyword Research & Onsite Optimization

Keyword research allows us to determine the best phrases to target in terms of visibility. We look for a balance of keyword phrases that are high in traffic, but not too competitive, so it is easier to become visible on major search engines. This is for the business owner or organization who wants the peace of mind of knowing they are using the best keyword phrases on their website to increase their visibility. By having the most effective keyword phrases properly integrated into your website, you'll see increased visibility and traffic.

To determine the keywords that are best suited for your site and your business, some research and analysis is required. The best place to do research on keywords and utilize webmaster tools to help you better understand and market your website is www.googlekeywordtool.com.

Search Engine Optimization (SEO)

Search engine optimization changes all the time. Make sure your provider is performing all "white-hat" SEO methods, as to not risk your overall listing with Google and other search engines by performing "black-hat" (unethical) SEO methods that may get your website up higher quicker, but not for long.

SEO is for the business owner or organization who wants increased visibility organically on the search engines (the left hand side of Google, Yahoo, Bing, etc., *not* the paid listings on the right). More visibility leads to more traffic, which means more leads if your website is properly designed with landing page optimization in mind. A properly designed site can help turn visitors into customers.

SEO can take four months or more before you see results in terms of a higher ranking for keyword phrases on the search engines. Additionally, keyword research needs to be completed prior to hiring an SEO specialist. The keyword research will determine if a specific SEO package will be sufficient or whether a more customized program is needed.

There are no guarantees any service will bring your site to the top of the search engines. Instead, ask the prospective search engine optimization company to show you case studies in which they have helped businesses rise to the top of the search engines. There are many companies dedicated to working only with SEO for businesses and websites, but often it is better to work with a company who also manages your website from an efficiency perspective.

SEO and keywords, however, are only one way to increase your site's visibility and generate more traffic. Let's take a closer look at some of the other ways to accomplish this.

PPC Management

PPC stands for pay-per-click. This means you only pay the search engine when someone clicks on your ad. Depending on your industry and how well your campaign is set up, this can yield tremendous ROI. Unlike search engine optimization services, you can guarantee your placement on search engines if your daily budget is high enough to display your ads all day.

We recommend starting with Google Adwords and if this proves to be successful, replicating these ads with Yahoo!, Bing, and possibly other paid advertising websites. Yahoo! and Bing are on the same platform so you can manage the advertising of both within one console website. Google Adwords provides better tools and trend tracking, hence the reason to start with Google Adwords and then add other paid advertising websites down the road.

If a third party is managing your Google Adwords or Yahoo!/Bing advertising campaigns, I recommend paying directly for the cost of the ads. This way you know exactly what you are spending and the management company isn't marking up the cost of the ads – or worse, not placing the ads. You should pay the management company simply for their time of managing the campaign to be the most effective.

The daily and monthly budget is best determined by investing $500 initially with Google and tracking this budget during the first month or until the money runs out. You can then extrapolate the data to determine how long your ads will display and how much of a budget will be required for your ads to be visible 24/7. The industry you are in and how competitive the keyword phrases are will determine the monthly budget needed. I have seen local and national campaigns from $100 per month in advertising spent to $10,000 or more in monthly advertising spent. It depends on your business and ROI as to whether this can be an effective use of advertising dollars.

Once effectively advertising on Google, it makes sense to duplicate the campaigns on Yahoo/Bing, which can be managed on the same platform.

In short, with PPC you only pay when someone is searching for and interested in the products or services you have to offer and clicks on your ad.

Directory Submissions with Google+ Local

Directories are basically online Yellow Pages that list businesses and websites. The more directories you are in and the more comprehensive your listing in each directory, the better your overall search engine ranking will be.

This is for the business owner or organization who wants increased visibility and to ensure they are listed on the major directories, which also helps in overall search engine rankings.

Being listed on the major directories with thorough listings will increase your visibility on search engines. The search engines will see that your business is listed on major directories, giving you more credibility. Your company will look superior to competitors that are not listed in the directories, or who are listed but do not have thorough listings. The value of directory submissions is not being listed in obscure directories that people don't typically use; the value is the major search engines such as Google, Yahoo!, Bing, etc., will see your business listed in these directories and increase your search engine ranking.

You can hire a company to submit your business to these directories, or you can submit them yourself. Some of the major directories to look at and publish your listing on are Yelp, Manta, Google+ Local, LinkedIn, Bing, Yahoo!, Merchant Circle, YellowPages.com, MapQuest, and Local.com, in no particular order. Of course the process will be slightly different for each of these directories and there's quite a bit of legwork. This list will get you started. The key is to make sure your information is consistent, thorough, and accurate. For example, if you use St. for an abbreviation of Street, you should use St. in all listings.

Moreover, I recommend one paid listing to ubl.org (Universal Business Listing). This service helps submit your listing to multiple directories automatically. There is a nominal annual fee, but it is highly recommended to push your listing out to a majority of directories.

Your overall online visibility will increase as more people will be able to find you.

Facebook Advertising

Facebook advertising allows you to target specific demographics. When people create their Facebook profile they typically put in their birthday (age), town they live in (location), gender, employment (what they do), interests and hobbies (what they like), and more. Clearly this is useful information for ad placement, as ads can be highly targeted and specific. As marketers, we use this information to create targeted ads for targeted audiences.

Facebook's pricing is determined by cost-per-click (CPC) or cost-per-thousand impressions (CPM). You can determine which method is best based on testing. You pay Facebook directly for the cost of the ads. Based on experience, I have found Facebook advertising to be successful for low-cost general branding.

Again, you can hire a professional company to do this for you, or you can simply go to your Facebook page for your business. If you don't have one yet, we'll cover social media in the next chapter.

Once you're on your page's dashboard or profile, you'll see a link to create a Facebook ad that looks just like an existing Facebook ad but with your page already on it. Click this ad and walk through the steps on the following page to fill out all the necessary information, select your demographic requirements, and determine what kind of ad you want to place (CPC or CPM).

The process of honing your ad placement and marketing skills can be a little time-consuming and tedious, but you can determine which way is more effective by trying one at a time or by running two campaigns at the same time. One thing to keep in mind is that if your product or service isn't something that a lot of people will click on right away, you may want to go with the CPC option to get more exposure at first. It often takes a number of times before someone will click on an ad, so paying per 1000 impressions may not be the best idea. It all depends on the campaign and your product, business, or service.

Ad Retargeting

Ad retargeting is a form of advertising that allows you to continue marketing to your audience after they've left your website. Only an average 2% of site visitors convert on their first visit, so you can see how useful this type of advertising can be; it allows you a second chance to convert the other 98%. Obviously if someone is already visiting your website, they already know your brand and have shown an interest. This is why retargeting is so effective.

Retargeting is a cookie-based technology. You place a small amount of JavaScript into your website that tags your website visitors and your ads essentially follow them across the web. You can integrate this with Google (they refer to it as remarketing) and increase your ROI.

How retargeting works in simple terms: you go to a website and it drops a cookie to follow the sites you're visiting. This cookie doesn't capture any other information. When you go to a new site, there's an automated process that takes place: the cookie notifies your retargeter when the visitor goes to another site. If there's ad space available on that site, your retargeter bids on it. If the bid wins, your ad appears on the site. All of this happens before the page loads.

Technology is pretty amazing! Now that we've talked about ads and generating traffic, it's time to cover one of the most popular ways of networking and marketing: social media. Social media marketing is highly effective and people trust it because you usually only share things you like or support with your friends.

Let's take a closer look at how social media marketing works and how it can help your business and marketing plan.

Chapter Ten
Social Media Marketing

For many, social media has become part of their everyday lives. For the past few years, Facebook, Twitter, Pinterest, YouTube, and other social media platforms have been growing in popularity and consistent usage. Businesses and individuals are especially utilizing Facebook and Twitter to get their products and services out there in front of their fans and target audiences. Additionally, building an audience is much easier online than it is offline.

Part of the reason this is so popular is because it allows fans and followers to interact with whomever they are following. If a business owner is active on social media and directly speaking to a number of people, this makes them more personable and easier to engage with over multiple platforms. Gone are the days of successful people being unreachable by the general population; now, we're seeing interactions between highly successful business people, authors, and musicians and their fans taking place all over social media platforms.

Customers are also using social media to complain about customer service or problems they have experienced with companies. Additionally, they are using social media to recommend and share with friends businesses with which they have had great experiences. Therefore, it is imperative to listen to what people may be saying about your brand or business.

So which social media platforms should you use as a business owner? Currently, the three main platforms are Facebook, Twitter, and YouTube. They're easy to use and easy to update, not to mention they make it easy for people to find you if your settings are set up correctly.

Facebook

Facebook is one of the largest and most popular social media platforms online today, and for good reason. Even though they've had their issues with privacy settings and other changes, they still manage to remain popular and keep their members (sometimes begrudgingly) coming back.

On Facebook, there are many options for marketing, networking, and advertising. For a business, you should create a Facebook page and begin collecting "likes" to form an audience. Once you have at least 400 "likes," you can use your page to offer specials and do other promotional activities like giveaways.

Other features on Facebook are ads, which can be highly targeted to a specific audience. You can input your audience's interests, age group, location, and other parameters to make the most of your ad. You can take the demographic information of your ideal customers and target ads specifically to these people. Furthermore, you can specify in your ad creation process that "liking" the ad itself will allow the person to "like" your Facebook business page without leaving where they currently are on Facebook.

When using Facebook advertising remember to create at least two ads in order to perform split testing. This allows you to test the ads, as one ad will almost always outperform the other. Moreover, don't forget that you can use multiple ads with tweaks to different demographics. For example, one ad could be targeted towards females, while the other could be targeted towards males.

Recently, they added a feature that allows you to promote a

specific post for several days for only $7. This will increase the chances of the post appearing on everyone's newsfeed throughout the days the promotion is paid for. Though this won't get you new page "likes" directly like an ad, it will ensure that everyone on your friends list and everyone who has "liked" your page is more apt to see your post. This can be very useful if you have a large number of friends and "likes" already on your business Facebook page and want to encourage the sharing of specific posts.

Twitter

Twitter has grown rapidly in recent years and is used by a number of people to update their followers in 140-character blurbs. There are a few reasons why this is a good thing, why it works, and why people love it. First, it's easy to update. Only being able to use 140 characters takes a little getting used to, but once you do, it's a great way to share what's going on in short, sweet posts. Hashtags allow you to keep up on trending topics, you can speak directly to one person with direct replies, and you can send direct, private messages. People can also retweet things they like, which encourages new followers, as well as interactions between you or your business and people who want to know what you're up to.

Twitter is a good way to build a following and share updates and links. If you have a Twitter marketing plan, you will likely post multiple updates within a day at peak times, as many people are on Twitter throughout the day. Regardless of when you choose to use it, Twitter is a good way to keep things short and simple while still promoting your work, company, and products.

You can also simply link your Facebook fan page to your Twitter page. Any posts that are posted on your Facebook fan page will feed to your Twitter page automatically. If your Facebook post is longer than 140 characters, Twitter simply truncates the message and links over to the full Facebook post.

Blogging

There are a number of people who are making money simply by blogging. For your business, however, your blogs should be informative, educational, and helpful to your site visitors.

If your visitors are existing clients or customers, chances are they're looking for something on your site. There's nothing better than free information and education. If your blog offers informative posts and videos, you can expect your site visitors will appreciate the content.

As the expert in your field, use that to your advantage by posting blogs that are educational and useful to your target audience. If they learn something from you, they are more likely to trust you and remember you. They will be more likely to come back to learn more. Remember: make sure your content has value. The first thing people are thinking about when they visit a website is, *What's in it for me?*

Depending on your area of expertise, you can break down each topic to its most essential information and focus on one or two areas per blog post. If your topic is marketing, for example, you can do a blog about choosing keywords and another about using backlinks. From there, you can move on to more traditional media and promotional items like bracelets, magnets, and bookmarks or pens. The smaller the topics you can brainstorm and write about, the more blog posts you'll have and the more educational your blog will be.

If your website is built on the WordPress platform it will be easy to post blogs. By having your blogs posted directly on your website, this will help your website rank higher on search engines. If your website doesn't have the capability, there are free blogging services you can use to post your articles to. However, by posting your blog articles within your own website, you will help increase your website's overall ranking.

Blogging is also a good way to make sure that your website is updated regularly. Every time you post fresh content, your site is updated and search engines like that, so it improves your ranking. What's not to like? You can then promote your new blog post by sharing the post with your Facebook fans and Twitter followers.

How Can a Blog Help My Marketing?

When it comes to online marketing, the strategies that worked just a few years ago have been nullified by updates in major search engine algorithms. No longer is it acceptable to simply spam keywords across a webpage and hope for the best. Neither can you spam your link across dead blogs and message boards in order to increase the quantity of inbound links to your website in hopes that simply having more links than the competition will raise your position in major search engines. Today, content is king and any content that you can produce that is relevant to your audience is helping your cause.

This content must not only be informative, but it must also be entertaining and delivered to the audience with a unique voice. No matter the industry, there are always competitors who are getting out ahead of you when it comes to breaking news and new tips. When you are not first with the latest industry news, you need to be the website that people go to for a humorous or unique take on whatever it is you're writing about.

Your content also needs to be dynamic. Static content creates short-term effects in the search listings of major search engines. Dynamic content, like the audience you are serving, is always moving in the direction of more relevant and more recent.

One of the most effective ways to incorporate this type of dynamic content into your marketing efforts in an organized fashion is through a blog. Blogging has proven itself to be quite effective when it comes to building and maintaining an audience and eventually converting them into loyal customers. However, there are some things you should know about blogging, how blogging can help your marketing, and how to correctly incorporate the strategies into your own blog. Below are a few tips on why you should begin a blog to help your marketing.

1. Blogs will help you to organize your thoughts in a way that customers can easily understand in a non-selling environment.

Because you will have to figure out the organizational structure for your blog before you actually begin producing content, you will naturally create a more effective organizational structure for that content. Your audience does not want to have to search through endless text to find the solution they are looking for. The process of beginning a blog will help you to organize your entire website so your audience can easily find the topics that interest them.

2. As you organize your blog, your website will become easier for major search engines to index.

One of the major components of a high rank in major search engines is the analytic of "stickiness," or how long a web visitor stays on your website once they have clicked through to it. The more organized your website is, the longer your audience will stay. The longer your audience stays, the more juice you gain with major search engines. Your website will then be ranked higher and viewed more often for the keywords which you optimized for.

3. You will create internal links and a linking structure that will help you in your search engine optimization.

Even if you know nothing about keyword optimization and building links, you will naturally create these as you create your blog entries. The more related keywords you have within the text on your website, the more search engines will associate your website with the content you are promoting. This will cause your website to rise in the rankings of major search engines, increasing your overall visibility online.

If you do know a little bit about keyword optimization and link building, you can do yourself a great service by linking articles to each other as they are related and creating an optimized keyword article for a particular topic of popularity. There are many online resources that you can use to learn about keyword optimization and link building. One resource is Google Trends (www.Google.com/trends), which allows you to type in a phrase and show you the overall level of interest and historical search pattern for that particular search phrase. Also, it will show the fastest rising related search phrases in terms of the number of people searching for more specific phrases.

4. You will be seen as an expert to leaders in social circles.

In order to increase your market share among individuals who know your industry, you must be seen as an expert in that industry. A blog can go a long way in helping to cultivate that image for you.

If you are the only one talking about certain topics, you will naturally be seen as an expert (as long as your solutions are correct). Even if you are not the only one talking about a certain topic, if you have information that other websites do not have, people will naturally come to you for the inside track on what is supposed to be happening.

Once you build a reputation within a community of people who are interested in your industry anyway, you will begin to find that your public relations will improve. People will begin recommending their friends to your website without having to directly market to them.

5. A blog creates a FAQ that can be used for customer service.

Customers like to know they are being taken care of at all times. A blog can serve not only as a source of dynamic content for search engine optimization, but also as a FAQ that your customers can access for solutions to problems that you can solve. Once people view you as this type of resource, you will also see your sales and revenue increase.

With a constantly expanding online FAQ, you'll free up your time from answering common questions you already answered online. Remember, your time is valuable! In time, you will be able to direct people to your online resources and direct your customer service energies into other parts of your business. Once this happens, you will have the time, energy, and manpower to expand your business to new customers instead of having to constantly take care of the problems with the customers that you already have.

Email Marketing

Email marketing has proven to be one of the fastest, most cost-effective ways to communicate with your clients. You can use email marketing to make announcements, such as new products or specials, and to inform your clients of changes that are coming or that have been made. Everyone is on email and most people check it every day, especially when they own a business. That makes email newsletters and announcements a great way to stay in touch with your customers and clients while keeping it convenient for them.

Newsletters take HTML and graphic skills to layout properly. It's a good idea to have some knowledge of that or be able to work around it with a platform like MailChimp, Constant Contact, Infusionsoft, etc. The more you keep your customers informed, the better your relationship and the more services and products they will purchase from you. Additionally, the more professional and consistent to your branding your newsletters are, the better your conversions will be.

If you want to do this yourself cost-effectively, you first have to have an email list to send the newsletters to. When you're first starting out, or even if you already have a list and just want to learn the process, one program to use online that works well and is free to use until you have a larger list is MailChimp. They have a drag and drop editor for creating your newsletters, allowing you to easily create sign up forms which can then be pasted directly into your site.

This is ideal for the small business that is just starting or for the do-it-yourselfer who wants to know each aspect of their business inside and out before handing off the task. In any case, email marketing should be a part of your marketing strategy in order to grow your business.

Text Messaging/SMS

Over 90% of text messages are read within one minute. Though not everyone likes being marketed to via text, it is becoming more common and a number of people do sign up for it. Typically your raving fans are the most likely to opt-in for text message updates. This group is also the most likely to buy from you.

Announcements and new product launches are two examples of what can be sent out with a text/SMS message to your customers. It's a simple, fast, and effective way to communicate with your clients and customers in a short message and to ensure they'll receive it. Chances are they will also read it almost immediately, which makes this a highly effective marketing tool.

There are a number of ways to do this, including hiring a company to do it for you or sending out a text blast yourself. Since this is relatively new, there are not as many resources online for this process as there are for newsletters, but the services out there operate about the same way. If your list of numbers is small, you can use a blast messaging service to send messages for little to no cost to you through certain websites. Once your list of subscribers increases in size, you will likely have to pay a fee for future messages.

The more you keep your customers informed, the better your relationship and the more services and products they will purchase from you. Text messages help ensure your message is read.

YouTube / Video Marketing

One of the best ways to communicate to people is through video. Video allows viewers to feel emotion and be more engaged with you. Moreover, you can easily build bonding and rapport through video and help people feel more comfortable. Additionally, video allows you to build credibility and trust. Once people trust you, they will feel more comfortable buying from you.

One of the biggest advantages of video is the ability to leverage your time. You shoot the video once and thousands or more people can watch that video over and over again. With social media networks such as YouTube and Facebook, video can be shared very easily. What's more is video is getting easier and cheaper to produce. In fact, you can create your own TV show right on YouTube.

A common question I get asked is, "How will I create content for videos?" I studied one of the world's top Internet marketers, Mike Koenigs, and he shared the content creation strategy of the 10x10x4. The 10x10x4 is the top 10 frequently asked questions your clients ask you and the top 10 questions your clients should ask you, but typically don't know enough about your industry to ask. The other four videos are related to the opt-in process of getting prospects to provide their email address. In short, with the bandwidth and technology we have today, video marketing should be a part of every small business owner's marketing plan.

Chapter Eleven
Direct Mail

Because so many people are moving their marketing efforts online and most companies do not send out unique direct mail, this gives innovative entrepreneurs a major advantage against the competition.

Online marketing is great and cost-effective, but to truly get through the clutter of ads and marketing messages people see on a constant basis, it's a good idea to compliment your online marketing with direct mail pieces.

Newsletters

A monthly printed newsletter is a great way to make it through the clutter. The large majority of small businesses do not offer a printed newsletter. Newsletters provide great value to build the relationship with your clients and even offer upsell opportunities.

Now, here's the best news: you'll make it through the clutter with a newsletter, by giving away value for free which builds your relationship with your customer over time, and hopefully some of your customers give your newsletters to others who might have an interest after they're done reading it, which could easily lead to more business.

Though there is some work required, once you get into the swing of it and have a system in place for creating these newsletters, it will take less and less time as you perfect the process. Also, there are done-for-you newsletter services. However, you still want to be sure your newsletter is personalized and doesn't look like a template. Overall, printing a newsletter isn't very expensive, so sending one out every month to your customers is a good investment in their value.

Multi-Step Direct Mail Sequence

Of all the ways to market and stay in touch with your customers or attract new customers, this is by far one of my favorites. Simply sending a postcard or letter isn't enough anymore. No matter what your endeavor, you have to get through your customers' daily clutter of mail and be unique. Standing out from the crowd will ensure that you make the biggest impact with your existing and future customers.

A big part of doing this is through sending unique things, for example 3D mailers. A 3D mailer gives you a chance to use an item – a novelty – and make your mail stand apart from all the other 2D mail. A flat piece of paper or postcard just doesn't cut it anymore, so why not add an item like a compass, with the headline, "Are You Lost When It Comes to XYZ? Use This Compass To Navigate Your Way To ABC Company." Or a boomerang with a headline that says, "We Want You To Come Back." Or a miniature trash can, with a headline like, "Don't Throw Away This Opportunity." Or a sales letter that is mailed in a bank bag with the headline, "You Can Take This To The Bank! Your XYZ Is Your Most Important Asset!" The possibilities are endless. These are all examples of 3D mail pieces that my company has sent out, and have made a huge difference in terms of getting through the clutter. If you recall from earlier in the book, we've seen returns of over 1000% utilizing 3D direct mail campaigns.

Having said that, here's something else to think about. What kind of four-step mailer program could you implement for *your* business? What kinds of items could you send with these mailers to get through the clutter to sell your products or services? How will this help your business get more customers and make you stand out from the crowd?

If you take the time to develop a mailer specifically targeting your ideal clients, then there's a good chance it will be successful. Since most customers need to be reminded at least three to seven times before purchasing, a multi-step mailer program is perfect. Additionally, when you find a winning sales letter, it is very easy to scale that marketing piece to similar people throughout your market.

Chapter Twelve
Public Relations (PR)

PR today is about content creation and overall community relations. You need PR that compliments social media and interacts with social networks just as well as with the traditional media players.

The PR industry has changed dramatically over the last five years. Today, it's much broader than simply writing press releases and generating clips. PR has evolved to become the cornerstone in helping companies reach and engage with their buyers and other key audiences in social medias and networks. Contemporary PR helps build communities that are passionate about your company's brand, and provides creative, authentic content that engages and inspires dialogue.

Advantages:

- Repositioning your business for growth
- Relationship building with your current and prospective clientele
- Building and strengthening your brand
- Building trust and loyalty
- Lead generation
- Building reputation and crisis management

Types:

- Announcements of changes, accomplishments, or awards to media and trades
  - ✓ Informational releases to local media
  - ✓ Informational releases to national media
  - ✓ Informational releases to trade publications
- Securing radio or TV interviews and appearances

✧ Event planning and compliance

In addition to traditional and blogger relations programs, forward-looking companies are starting to think like publishers themselves – sharing ideas, spurring conversations, engaging in industry trends, and developing valuable digital marketing content that helps propel their brands. That means reaching and engaging your customers on a personal level with authentic, relevant content that can be easily found and shared through your website, blog, and across social networks. The development of original content also dramatically improves your SEO rankings and marketing efforts, which ultimately generates more leads and sales. Having your company published in newspapers, trade publications, being on TV, or being in radio interviews is much more valuable than purchasing ads directly with the media.

To get your business, new product, or announcement out into the world through a press release, your first step is to *write* the press release. If you're using a free press distribution site such as PRLog.org, be sure to follow their press release writing guidelines before creating your first draft. This goes for other press release sites, too, such as PR Splash, Briefing Wire, and Pitch Engine. Many of these sites offer a basic service for free and an extended service for a fee.

So how do you write a press release, anyway? Let's face it: business owners often simply don't have the time to do these themselves, so they hire a freelance writer to do it for them. Whether you choose to dive in and write your own release or hire someone to do it for you, here are some basic rules about press releases.

First, your press release has to appeal to the media. What

they're looking for isn't about you or your business. They don't care if their piece will help you promote your website or business. What a reporter wants is a story that will be interesting for their readers and that the editor will love and ultimately publish.

So, the first thing to think about is how you can make your announcement sound newsworthy and get the attention of a reporter or journalist. The headline and subhead are the most important parts. If you don't get their attention there, you probably won't in the rest of the release, as they most likely won't even look at it.

Here's something to remember for your headline and subhead: it has to be direct, to the point, and about a topic (your story) that strikes people as important or worth reading about. You can dig around online and do some research elsewhere to discover your angle, or what your focus will be in presenting your business, product, or service.

Once you have a good title and subhead, it's time to write the press release lead. This is essentially the introduction to your press release that further explains the title and subhead. The main components of a press release lead are the who, the what, the where, the when, and the how. This should give the reader enough information to understand the basics of the story.

In the rest of the press release, you can elaborate on some of the key pieces of information and back up whatever was said in the title, subhead, and lead. You should consider adding quotes from relevant sources and any studies or research that compliments your story.

Next, it's appropriate to write a sentence or two about your company and what you do. Be sure to include your website address. If your press release is published on an online news website, the link to your website will easily help readers contact you and the link to your website will also help your overall search engine ranking. Once you have this completed, a set of three hashtags (# # #) signifies the end of the press release. Be sure to add contact information just below the hashtags so anyone who is interested can get in touch with you.

In terms of getting your press release published, you should submit your press release directly to a specific contact at the respective media source and via fax whenever possible. The media receives so many press releases via email and online distribution services, a faxed press release will stand out. Then, utilize a digital press release distribution service such as PR Newswire that will distribute your press release online. This service generally will help you increase your website's search engine ranking, especially if you include your website address in the article.

Some basics to keep in mind about press releases as you're writing are to avoid hype words (state of the art, breakthrough), never write in first person unless it's a quote, and keep the press release as short as possible while still including all relevant information. All that's left is giving it a shot – let's see those press release writing skills!

Chapter Thirteen
Integrating with Traditional Media

Online marketing may be the new thing, but traditional media is still there and still remains a viable option for every business, especially if you know how to call people to action.

In chapter six, we discussed lead generation magnets and how to connect people to your website from traditional media ads. We'll be focusing on that again in this chapter.

Your lead generation magnet could be anything of value that the customer can obtain for free. People now *expect* to get free information that is valuable because the Internet is a wealth of useful (and not so useful) information. This is why you have to provide something of value to give your potential customers for free so you can begin to build trust and make them want more from you.

With your lead generation magnet in mind, let's explore some of your options for advertising through more traditional mediums.

Yellow Pages

Though you may feel that no one uses the Yellow Pages anymore, there are still a number of people who use them, especially locally. If your business is listed, you have the opportunity for prospects to see your listing. If you aren't listed, your prospects definitely won't find you. If you have a location – any location – or a product, service, or offer you want to share, having a listing in the Yellow Pages is a good way to reach those who might not be reachable through the Internet.

Besides that, wouldn't it be better to have a listing and increase visibility that way rather than not having a listing and a potential client slip through and go with a competitor who *is* listed?

Billboards

Billboards are still widely in use and can be a highly useful marketing tool. Though billboards can work better for some businesses than others, a billboard allows you to display a giant message – which also means you have the opportunity to display a giant call to action or lead generation magnet.

This medium can also connect you with prospects and clients who may not be available online regularly. Maybe they're too busy traveling to try to search the web, or maybe they don't have a laptop? There are people who aren't tech-savvy, so if your business is trying to reach an audience who may or may not be online, this is another great media.

TV

Even with Netflix and Hulu and YouTube and Crackle, people do still enjoy local television and shows that aren't yet available through those other services. When it comes to TV, people like to know what's going on in their neighborhoods and local areas so they can plan for weather, traffic, and events in the area they live. Local news also often includes publication announcements, happenings, and businesses that are doing something unique.

If you're unable to get your business on the news, maybe it's time to consider taking out a TV ad. Videos are fairly easy to make these days and every TV station still shows ads in order to keep their revenue up and help support the station. Depending on how many viewers the station has, TV can be a very cost-effective media.

Radio

Everyone loves music and listening can be done while doing other things. This is why radio is still so important: music and radio shows are fun, easy to participate in as a listener, and easy to enjoy. The radio is a great place to advertise, locally or nationally, through Internet radio or through more traditional radio.

As long as you have your call to action here, too, you'll be able to sneak into people's thoughts through their ears and plant a seed. Maybe they don't even need your services but their friend brings up a problem you and your business can solve the day after they hear an ad. They'll remember and make the suggestion to their friend, which merges radio and word-of-mouth advertising.

Newspaper

Newspapers are definitely not as popular as they once were, but there are a large number of people who still enjoy reading the newspaper with their morning coffee. Even if not on paper, a lot of news publications are now available online or in tablet formats, so advertising in a newspaper still works. Often, newspapers will bundle print advertising with online advertising. In fact, if they do publish to tablets and in eBook formats, you can add links to your ad as well.

If someone is still reading the news in paper format, you can still utilize your call to action or lead magnet to get them to visit your website and take advantage of obtaining something for free. After that it just depends on the experience they have on your site and whether the information they found there was useful or valuable to them or not.

As you can see, integrating each media with the online world is a great way to increase visibility and acquire more customers than just using one of the above or only the Internet. Further, if all of your ads have a common thread – like your logo or slogan – then people will begin to recognize and become familiar with your brand before they even become a customer or visit your site.

Finally, *all of these mediums together lead to greater visibility*. Recall the statements about how many ads someone sees in a day and how many "touches" it takes to reach a customer and make them take action. All of these traditional medias combined in an integrated way can drive more customers to your business simply because they see it multiple times and begin to become familiar with your brand.

All of these medias can also use direct response marketing to increase leads. Direct response marketing is essentially removing the middle man. For example, if you sell a product through a handful of retailers but would like to measure more precisely where your customers are coming from, simply market for your business and have the customers buy directly from you instead of another retailer.

Not only does this allow you to measure where people are coming from and what they're hearing about you; it also allows you to establish a direct line of communication with your customers. Depending on your business and how established you are, this means that people feel more special and subconsciously may feel slightly obligated to either send you a referral or purchase a product or service.

Chapter Fourteen
Finalizing Your Plan & Taking Action

This is the best part! I hope you've read through the chapters and gained some useful insight into business, marketing, and tips to grow your organization and get more customers. I also hope you see the importance of providing value for your potential customers, even if they haven't purchased anything just yet.

In this section, I'll recap what was covered. I'd like for you to create a table and brainstorm the best marketing options for you, as well as what your budget for each will be. This is an exercise of practice, as well as a tool for revision and planning; implementing the final version of your marketing plan and calendar – the table we'll be creating a draft of in this chapter – will empower your business and expand your horizons.

But first, let's review.

Chapter one was my story of starting my business at fifteen years old and how my business has grown into a full service marketing company.

Chapter two was about goals and your customer's worth. We discussed how you should begin by having an endgame and how your business expansion will never be possible without your customers.

Important points to remember:
- ✓ Your endgame should always play a part in what you're working towards.
- ✓ Your customer is priceless – without customers, you have no profit. No profit

means no business.
- ✓ Keep your marketing efforts focused.

Chapter three was essentially an introduction to the idea of a marketing plan and calendar. One of the most important things to keep in mind when creating these documents is: how will you get through the clutter?

Important points to remember:
- ✓ Your prospect must be "touched" at least three times before they buy.
- ✓ Your marketing should stand apart from the crowd to get through the clutter.
- ✓ If your marketing cost brings back a customer whose lifetime value exceeds the cost of the marketing, you get a worthwhile return on investment.

Chapter four was all about building your brand. This includes your business name, logo, mission, vision, and customer service habits. Branding also includes reputation marketing, which can be easier if your brand is associated with positives in all aforementioned categories.

Important points to remember:
- ✓ Your business name should communicate what your business offers.
- ✓ Your logo should be easily recognizable and reproduce in color or black and white.
- ✓ Your brand covers every aspect of how your business is presented and perceived by the public.

Chapter five was all about your website. Having a positive and professional web presence can get you new clients, as well as be a bridge to your local customers. People tend to search the Internet for directions, ideas, products, and services, so having a website for your business is necessary.

Important points to remember:
- ✓ Your web presence is part of your brand and reputation.
- ✓ There are many different types of websites, so figure out which type suits your business the best.
- ✓ Monitoring web traffic is a good indicator of where your attention should be focused.
- ✓ Updating your site consistently makes it more valuable to search engines and more visible to people.

Chapter six provided a closer look at lead generation magnets. There are a number of different things you can create to serve as your lead generation magnets. The point is to get the potential client's email address so you can follow up and provide something of value. These serve as the three or more "touches" repeatedly mentioned throughout this book, which will increase the changes of the prospect making the decision to buy.

Important points to remember:
- ✓ Your lead generation magnet has to entice the visitor to trade his or her email for what you're offering.
- ✓ As long as you're providing something of value, the customer will respect it and come back for more.
- ✓ Combining multiple lead generation magnets to create a kit is your best bet for creating the most value for your potential customer.

Chapter seven was about utilizing video for your site and to reach your customers. Video makes you more "human" because you have a face to go with your name and voice; your business and speaking style will shine through when using video and make the customer's experience more personable.

Important points to remember:
- ✓ People are looking to connect with *people* and no one wants to feel like they're being sold to.
- ✓ Potential customers need to like the person behind the business to do business with them.
- ✓ Video allows your customers to get to know you even if you're asleep or in a meeting.

Chapter eight gave you an inside look at reputation marketing. This is one of the most important aspects. Customers now are generally web savvy and expect a certain rating from whomever they plan to do business with. Having no rating is just as bad as having a bad reputation, so managing how your company looks online is an important part of staying in business and succeeding.

Important points to remember:
- ✓ Your business reputation online can be tracked and corrected if some customers have left negative feedback.
- ✓ Customers pay attention to reviews and ratings and are influenced by them.
- ✓ Taking time to address a customer's complaint can inspire them to change their review and rating.
- ✓ Have a system in place to attract reviews and feedback from your clients. Ideally, one that triages the negative reviews so you can improve customer service internally, before

the reviews get published online.

Chapter nine provided details on how to generate traffic to your website. We covered everything from search engine optimization to ad retargeting, with many of these tools helping you to get people visiting your site and browsing its content.

Important points to remember:
- ✓ Building your online presence and getting the attention of those who are interested in your business takes time if you do it yourself.
- ✓ SEO and directory submissions can aid in your quest for generating relevant traffic to your site.
- ✓ Quality traffic is much more valuable than the quantity of traffic.

Chapter ten was all about social media. Social media is highly valuable to businesses because of its current impact on the masses. Who do you know that doesn't have Facebook, Twitter, or some other social media account? Even if they're still stuck in MySpace, they are still online. Social media is a powerful tool for business.

Important points to remember:
- ✓ Social media makes it easier for people to interact with whoever it is they're following, so be respectful, kind, and helpful to those who reach out to your business.
- ✓ Social media offers a wide variety of ad options.
- ✓ Social media for your business helps your website rank higher in search engines.
- ✓ Blogging is a multifaceted tool that helps with SEO as well as customer service.

Chapter eleven covered direct mail and how it can help your marketing efforts. By intertwining your web presence with your local presence, you are not only reaching a broader audience but also building your reputation and credibility online and offline.

Important points to remember:
- ✓ Just sending a postcard is no longer enough.
- ✓ Always provide value.
- ✓ Make sure your direct mail marketing is working together with your online marketing.
- ✓ Think outside the box with 3D mail campaigns and multiple-step campaigns.

Chapter twelve provided a closer look at public relations and how to write a basic press release. Public relations is important for a number of reasons. Being featured somewhere is much more effective and important than placing an ad.

Important points to remember:
- ✓ Being featured somewhere (in a newspaper, on the radio, or on TV) is much more effective than an ad and gives your business more credibility.
- ✓ Writing a press release or putting together a small press kit (physical or electronic) can be your gateway to being featured.
- ✓ PR repositions your business for growth and builds your brand as well as your reputation.

In chapter thirteen we explored integration into traditional media. Lead generation magnets were referenced again, as well as having a call to action in your ads through traditional media.

Important points to remember:

- ✓ A call to action or lead generation magnet will get you more leads.
- ✓ Using direct response marketing in conjunction with your ads allows you to measure your return and communicate directly with your customers.
- ✓ Prospective customers expect value for free now in order to learn if they can trust you.

Now that we've reviewed all of the chapters one more time and refreshed your memory, I want you to take out a piece of paper and a pen and start brainstorming. Think about some marketing ideas you can implement yourself or some services you're willing to purchase. Go ahead... stop reading and do this for at least 15 minutes.

....

Now that you've got some ideas, take a blank page and make a table with three columns. Title these three columns as follows:

Type of Marketing
What Month Do I Want to Implement This?
What is My Budget?

Congratulations! You now have your first draft of a marketing plan and calendar. Of course, you can revise and write it down more neatly, type it up, and even print it out to hang on your wall so you always know what's ahead. This brainstorming session and table are your foundation though, and will serve as a nice, solid one because you've learned a massive variety of different marketing techniques in this book.

Chapter Fifteen
Need Additional Help?

Jimmy Marketing can provide you help with implementing your marketing plan or consulting if you'd like to take a more direct route of learning. We look forward to hearing from you if this is the route you choose!

Main Office:
86 Boston Post Road #3
Waterford, CT 06385

Toll-free: 877.253.0273
Main: 860.442.9999

Fax: 860.910.4061

Hours:
9:30 AM to 4:30 PM EST Monday to Friday*
*We open at 11:30 AM on Thursdays as our weekly team training meeting takes place from 9:30 AM to 11:30 AM EST every Thursday.

Visit www.JimmyMarketing.com, www.EasyWebCreations.com, or www.JimmyConsulting.com to explore, learn, and get to know us even better.

Thank you for reading and I wish you the best of luck in attracting and increasing your leads; then converting those leads into sales which ultimately leads to more profits for you!

Made in the USA
San Bernardino, CA
02 October 2015